SILVER TONGUED DEVIL

Anthology

Rimes of The Ancient Mariner

SILVER TONGUED DEVIL

Anthology

Celebrating five years of outstanding East Village poetry,

fiction, memoirs, essays, storytelling, humor, and spoken word.
Compiled and edited by
Linda Kleinbub and Anthony C. Murphy

Pink Trees Press
New York, New York

Editors
  Linda Kleinbub
  Anthony C. Murphy

Contributing Editor
  Phillip Giambri

Cover Rendering
  Phillip Giambri

ISBN-13: 978-1-5136-7204-5
Pink Trees Press
New York, New York
Cover design Phillip Giambri
First Edition: December 2020

In Memory of

Matthew Abuelo
Pat Christiano
Steve Dalachinsky
Gil Fagiani

Foreword

by **Phillip Giambri** aka The Ancient Mariner

In 2013 writers were "beating the boards" on the open mic circuit (I called us Open Mic Gypsies) and had fewer and fewer opportunities for anything more than the standard five-minute open mic spot. Fifteen-minute "Features" were disappearing. It was mostly due to economics and is very understandable since poetry and writers notoriously do not generally inspire the public to rush out and buy tickets to events or meet even a two-drink minimum. It's a tough row to hoe for anyone artistically insane enough to try and produce these venues, but try I did.

"Rimes of The Ancient Mariner" was created to fill that ever-narrowing gap providing monthly spots for up to four featured performers, known as Silver Tongued Devils. All "Silver Tongued Devils" were personally and fairly selected by me for their writing skills, performance ability, and having paid their dues as "open mic gypsies." Featured performers also provided an important mentoring and training function in the open mic process. What I personally learned on open mic was gleaned by carefully watching and studying the featured performers I admired and talking to them about their work. I felt it provided both the opportunity to step up and a chance to learn for newcomers on the circuit. Our venue was funded by open mic signees and guests. Since this was strictly a not for profit operation, we felt that with the support of the open mic community and their friends, we could keep the fees reasonable.

Our featured performers were accorded the respect they deserved by having pre-show publicity, programs with bios and pictures, billed near the front of the show rather than at the end, which had been the standard at that time, insuring the event began on time allowing features and open mic readers to not feel pressured, and most importantly, a warm and welcoming environment to work in among like-minded and talented friends. A video was recorded of everyone who ever read at our show, was edited, and posted online as a valued learning tool for writers developing skills as "performance poets," breaking from the traditional stiff and cold poetry readings with artificial sounding "poets voice."

This fifth-anniversary anthology highlights sampled works of more than one hundred very talented writer/performers who featured at our show. They comprise a stunning cross-section of the most talented writers, poets, spoken word artists, storytellers, actors, and songwriters in the downtown New York City writing community; from theater, TV, Concerts, Academia, Cabarets, Clubs, bars, and anywhere that creative writing flourishes.

I feel blessed to have had the opportunity to meet, promote, and befriend these wonderfully talented artists.

A "Special Recognition Award" is long overdue to my tireless Rimes crew who made the magic look simple and me look like I knew what I was doing. To them and their hard work I owe any and all success:

    Anthony C. Murphy – Associate Producer, writer, poet
    Janet Restino – House Manager, Spoken Word Performer, artist
    Cal Reynolds – Bartender, musician, sculptor

Editors' Introductions

Linda Kleinbub "I was fairly new to reading my writing out loud and was always extremely nervous when doing so when I discovered The Rimes of the Ancient Mariner reading series hosted by The Ancient Mariner himself, Mr. Phillip Giambri. His welcoming demeanor immediately put me at ease. I returned month after month while working towards my MFA at The New School.

I was entering into a whole new world. I have been writing since I was a child and always kept my writing extremely private. I had zero experience reading my work aloud. While I was learning about writing in an academic environment, Phillip's show showed me what a writer's life was really about. His features were talented and provided learning tools to my student's toolbox. His audience was caring and attentive. Everyone loved the cozy, caring atmosphere that Phillip provided for writers.

I was always impressed by the diverse talent that graced the Ancient Mariner shows. I soon found out the Phillip attended open mics across the city always in search of talent, whether it be the polished actor turned poets, or the young nervous romantic pouring out her heart. Everyone was invited to read their work."

Anthony C. Murphy "When I first came to New York, in 2009, I thought it would be a whole different world. Like a movie. It isn't. We are similar.

I first met Phillip Giambri at an open mic downstairs at the old place on McDougall Street. 116. I think. In Greenwich Village. A place where Jimi and Bob Dylan had been. I was searching back then... then there was The Nuyorican and The Bowery round the corner... and there were good guys and gals who hosted and boosted us. There were other places with strange names: Jujo Mukti Tea Lounge, Tiki Lounges, St. Mark's, and always the sticky downstairs of somewheres.

I found something else that stuck with Phillip Giambri in a place called Bar 82, I think we just knew it wasn't all about us. Even though we still wanted to talk loudly and often.

I had been reading for a few years before in England but I was not confident. Standup comedy was king anyway. And what is a line without a punch?

We went to be heard. I think that is why we all went. We want to be heard. And it was open, so that meant all of us had a voice. We had to listen too."

Table of Contents

Rimes of The Ancient Mariner

MATTHEW ABUELO

Random Thoughts

Do the can collectors still hear the melody
Which comes before the steam heat hisses?
And will they waltz in St. Vitus' dance
Through the heavy metal doors?
Ruin is a rebirth
Or
An abortion.
The abortion is less cruel.
Have you realized
That heaven's watchman is absent
Not just for you
But for the Haitian kid buried under the latest storm
First announced on the 5 am news
And finds all his prayers
Were pleads to an empty room
He once thought full.
Do they,
The can collectors
Dream of seeing New York City from an airplane,
High above
Out of sight of for rent signs
Eviction notices
The wards and emergency rooms
Parades
Some which breakout in colors and languages
While others lead to drunken resentment,
Delis
And the gentrification of Spanish Harlem?
After all, if the pigeons can escape the sound of car horns
Which announce the boredom of those waiting to get through the Holland
tunnel...
And what is a city that hides behind an ocean of lights

30,000 feet below?
And have the shut-ins grown wary
Of the intrusion that comes through the radiators
Forcing them to open their windows
Onto an unloyal city they chose to escape
But never left at all?

NICHOLE ACOSTA

From 9/11 to 11/9

America just turned into one big locker room and I feel totally Naked and
Afraid
We gave The Biggest Loser The Voice

The Hoarders and Real Housewives are playing Storage Wars.
They're trading all their isms
they hid beneath floorboards.

We wish Ashton Kutcher would jump out of the bushes and tell us we just
got Punk'd
but this is The Real World
and Here Comes Honey Boo Boo
doing whatever he wants

I can't keep Keeping Up with the Kardashians
I don't feel like Dancing With The Stars
I am just a Nemo
in a tank full of sharks

We're stuck in Gordon's worst Kitchen Nightmare with Pence as The
Apprentice
We're all Extreme Couponing
because Freedom is expensive

Join me on the next season of
Survivor.

AUSTIN ALEXIS

Needs

She wanted a lover,
one who would not give her any diseases,
who would not resent her successes,
who wouldn't turn into a gargoyle
or a moon desert or a mirage,
one who would teach her
how to relax and enjoy the world,
one who would be there for her
at her life's inevitable sunset.
But when he finally arrived,
lit up with green and easefulness,
she sensed something else she craved
was missing…a thing
she couldn't name or even envision.

BARBARA ALIPRANTIS

A Baby Sees

In 1980, I entered the world of the Deaf and Hard of Hearing by accepting a position as the Resident Storyteller at St. Joseph's School for the Deaf, Bronx, NY, and learned to communicate in sign language – on the job. In 1985, I took a workshop intensive with the National Theatre of the Deaf, and went on to teach Sign Language thru storytelling and became a lifelong advocate for the Deaf and all people with disabilities.

The poem, "A Baby Sees" was inspired by a 9-year old boy named George. I was facilitating a Pantomime Workshop and his assignment was to show us– without using sign language OR mime– that he was a doctor. He signed a tiny story that touched my heart and when I sat down to record it, I wrote this poem.

A Baby Sees...

Once upon a time a baby was born,
And the world was a happy place…
Mom and Dad were overjoyed,
As they welcomed their brand-new baby boy!

Baby smiled when he saw Mom's face,
The world indeed was a happy place.

Mom and Dad talked of their hopes and fears,
As they learned to deal with baby's tears,
"Is the baby hot? Is the baby cold?"
"Why won't he do what he's told?"
"Okay, so he's only six months old!"
While this baby's world was a happy place,
This baby's world was a quiet place…
And a day arrived when Mom's face changed.
Mom's face showed anguish,
Mom's face showed pain.

"What's wrong, what can it be?"

"I hope there's nothing wrong with me?"

They went for help as fast as they could,
They did everything any parent would…
"Dad looks so strange…Mom's so sad…"
"I hope it's not cause I've been bad?"

The doctor looked serious.
The doctor looked sad.
There was no question about it…
The news was bad.

From doctor to doctor the family went,
They went wherever they were sent…
They hoped for the best,
But, the story stayed the same:

"I'm sorry, Mom, your baby can't hear…"
"My baby is deaf, is that what you mean?"
While the baby could not hear her voice,
He saw her scream!
He saw the grief upon her face,
And the world was no longer a happy place.

"Something's wrong with me…what can it be
I can't understand what I see, but one thing's clear,
Something is wrong with me."

They talked behind him,
They talked to his face…
He could not hear the words,
But the message was clear:
"Something's wrong cause I can't hear."

He tried to make them understand.
He made faces; he moved his hands…

"Why are they crying when they look at me?
Don't they know that I can see
That's something's very wrong with me."

"How can I make them understand?
That I don't know why they can't love me
the way I am."

RICHARD ALLEN

West Texas Highway

On a west Texas highway, the bus barrels through midnight, under a slate of pure black canvas sky. I sit slumped and cramping, my face against the cold window. The occasional on-coming headlights splinter in the beads of rain that cling to the glass. In the high beams that barely reach out from the greyhound, hail falls like a constant shattered strand of pearls. The sound on the cab is one long deafening, barrage, an endless shotgun blast without power or purpose.

All lights are off, except for a single descending cone above a smoking Mexican. I stare blankly at the swirling exhales that drift up, giving the light new dimension. Our hook-nosed driver has no visible neck and three chins so that it looks like his head is melting into his shoulders. He hums some bouncy Irish jig loudly. It seems almost sadistic the way he goes on and on, on this torturous ride through the flatlands.

Feeling as if my head was inside a bell, hallucinating from withdrawal, I remember Willy Wonka's twisted boat ride and scream to myself, "No, daddy, I most certainly do not want a boat like this!" The hail halts suddenly and we pull into an El Paso rest stop.

Crossing the slick wet ground, a coke with no ice in hand, I see a small man with his pants down. He's feeding a payphone, his semi-erect dick visible in the edge of a street light. I watch as he hangs up and desperately fumbles for coins in the pockets of his fallen pants. Finally finding a quarter, he drops it in and scans the lot. Nobody there except for a guy drinking a coke with no ice. In the shadows he grins at me, turning his bare ass my way to finish his call.

Feeling like I'm in "Deliverance" without the benefit of a crossbow, I beat it (so to speak) post-haste into the stop, and shuffle past rows of twenty-five cent televisions and a cross-section of malformation, American style. Finding a men's room, I shut the stall and inspect the morsel of dope I have left. How did it come to this? I left New York with six hundred dollars of this shit; I grumble to myself. I prepare to finish it when the men's room door opens. An official pair of boots sits down next to me.

Injecting in a panic, I pull the needle from my arm as a drop of blood splats visibly on the white tile floor. Licking the blood quickly before more can fall, I look between the slats to see several servicemen having their hands blown from wall mounted dryers.

I make it to the bus and take my seat as pangs of fidgety anxiety surrender my knees. I know they'll be back with reinforcements. Air blows up my face as my head rests heavily against the window. I stare out as we leave and curse myself for not being sparing in my drug consumption. The plan was simple when I left New York. I had intended to whittle down the proverbial monkey on my back while seeing the heartland on a nod.

I had started out with six bundles. One was gone by the time we hit D.C. I wasn't looking too good, but I was feeling real well as the song goes, when the bus stopped in South Caroline to pick up an invasion of Marines from Paris Island. I guessed my long black hair and androgynous sensibilities caused me to look a bit like Cher when I heard from a few seats up a leatherneck hiss, "I wish I could sleep on a bus like that chick back there." Rather than correct him, I just continued to view signs for fireworks and pecan pies as we moved south along red clay foothills.

The sun was coming up as our path skirted Jacksonville, headed down I-95. We stopped at a station boasting an air-conditioned citrus stand and a giant billboard for Ron Jon's Surf wear. I crossed the parking lot on spindly legs and Cuban heels to the payphone to call my brother. I should be there in about an hour, I told him and hung up.

His El Camino kicked gravel as he pulled up, fresh out of prison from eight years on a work farm for not turning State's evidence. In the forty-minute drive to his house, I heard the story of his bust, of the shoeboxes of coke and currency buried in his yard and hidden in his closet. Due to absence, he was a brother I hardly knew. I felt bad that he got busted when he did. Only a few years later, the courts would have been jammed with drug cases and he might have done half the time, and maybe not lost his wife and son. But as I sat there looking at a face that I hadn't seen since the late seventies, a face that was mine in so many details, I fell blank with nothing to say. I had only come down to collect some money from my parents. The guilt I felt for bringing dope into his house while he was on parole manifested. It felt like the drugs I carried in my breast pocket thumped like a tell-tale heart.

The next morning over cold breakfast cereal, my brother told me that he had the money, but that mom and dad couldn't make it over to see me before I left. He asked if I was leaving that night with a hesitant smile and a nervous look. I nodded my head with an uneasy "Yes," and understood. Later, with my brother at work, I sat at the breakfast table after getting high, staring at a single cheerio floating in a plastic kiddy bowl, swollen and bloated with milk.

When he dropped me at the station, my brother gave me a forced hug that felt more like a shove. The sadness trickled out of his eyes like a summer sweat. He was looking at a kid brother he hardly knew, and most likely would never see again. As the bus left, tears came through the impregnable wall I'd constructed for myself. It seemed that the only way to patch the holes and not to feel was to double up on what was in my pocket.

The rest of the trip consisted of hypnotic injections in lavatories with opaque views of a world I did not understand, nor feel a part of. Leaving El Paso, we moved west as my sickness grew. I longed to be clean, to be new, to be a child whose only worry was a sunburn on his shoulders. I wanted to go out to dinner with my parents after a movie, and swipe the plastic saber of fruit from my mom's whiskey sour when she wasn't looking, only to have her shoot me back a sly smile.

The greyhound pulled into the station in Hollywood, and I reluctantly placed my foot on the ground. Escaping the bus, I was instantly sick of myself for returning here. My ex-wife met me and I could see she was doing pretty well for herself as she handed me several balloons of dope. I fixed in the back seat of her Barracuda. After the whole ordeal, even as the drugs took hold, I realized that they could no longer take me to a place free of pain. And I could actually see an end to this life.

MICHAEL ANTON

Subway Submissions

Part 1.

There is a man in late middle age seated across from me.

He is absorbed in a book with the title either Kama or Kaba; I can't quite make it out.

I cannot tell if he resembles the Russian composer Prokofiev, because I do not know what Prokofiev looked like. I suppose I could google Prokofiev and find out. The only classical composer whose features I am familiar with are Beethoven's. I think most people are like me in that regard.

He is wearing a red plaid woolen hunter's cap, and his glasses are perched atop his hat. Like me, he needs to remove his glasses in order to read.

His glasses have side things of plastic to protect his eyes, making them almost look like safety glasses.

Perhaps he works around machinery or power tools? Maybe a high school shop teacher?

Part 2.

I am standing by the door on the express side, which will not open for several stops when a mother and daughter Latina pair enter on Spring St. Mom: about 30, daughter about 12.

They sit down and take Lays Potato Chip bags from black plastic bags that they are each carrying. In a simultaneous movement, they both open their bags. The opening of the bags makes just one sound, not two. That's how highly synchronized it was.

Daughter: Barbequed chips. Mom: Sour cream and onion.

Part 3.

I am standing in front of the door. On the two-seater seat to my right is a middle-aged man reading a book whose language I cannot make out. It looks like it might be Cyrillic. Wait no! It's Arabic or Persian. No, it's Cyrillic!

I take my glasses off, thinking that will give me a sharper view.

It doesn't.

It seems to keep changing. The man is not reading on an electronic device, but a printed book.

Is it possible that printed matter on a page can keep shifting from Cyrillic to a Middle Eastern alphabet?

Part 4.

I am again standing by the door, and across from me is a young woman seated and reading a book that clearly is giving her great pleasure. She is smiling and positively glowing with each page.

But here's the odd thing. She has only the middle section of a paperback. Front and back covers, first and final chapters…all missing.

She turns a page, and it falls off. She is clearly done with this page. Rather than let it fall to the car floor, she stuffs it into her bag.

I respect that.

More pages will fall off. How do I know this? She is picking at the adhesive binding, which is exposed. The title wore off or fell off long ago. I'll never know what book she was reading that so entertained her, or why she had only the middle section.

She is reading, beaming, and picking at the glue, getting a piece off, and rolling it between her thumb and forefinger.

If I ever meet her, and we become friends, I'll buy her a new copy.

Part 5.

There is a stocky middle-aged African American fellow seated across from me.

It is a rainy day, and our car is nearly empty. There is plenty of room on the seats next to him for his backpack, but he has chosen to store it under his seat where the floor might be wet.

From the gold-edged pages, I can tell he is reading a bible. He is wearing a baseball cap that reads, "I Love Jesus". Between the words "love" and "Jesus" is a big red heart, so I guess it could be interpreted that he loves loves Jesus.

In his left hand he holds a yellow highlighter. He is clearly left-handed. He is using the highlighter on the pages of the bible but in an unusual way. He is not highlighting whole passages or even whole sentences. It looks like he is highlighting individual words or even letters, so swiftly does he lower it to the page and lift it up again.

It is almost as if he is tapping out Morse Code on the bible. Dot dot dot dash dash dot dash dot.

In real Morse Code it would look like this: …--.-.

His stop is approaching and he pulls from his knapsack a blue vinyl case with a handle that is only slightly larger than his bible. He then puts the bible into this case. It looks like a small briefcase that could accommodate only a bible or other similarly sized book. The case goes into the pack, the pack on his back, and he exits the train.

Part 6.

It is evening.

The couple are in their mid-forties, and clearly into each other. They have come from some kind of corporate event, as each one is carrying a swag bag that has printed on it NORTHEAST REGIONAL something or other. I get the feeling that they have known each other slightly before, and that perhaps each attended this event in the hope that the other would be there. He's Italian and she's Russian, so they are speaking in their only common language; English.

He tells her how hard it is to start dating again after a divorce, and she is sympathetic since she's also divorced, but also firm that he has to move on and put the past behind him.

It is evident that she would like to help him in this effort.

As my stop approaches, she looks him in the eye and asks shyly, "Please, what is your horror sign?"

Part 7.

Another evening.

He is a hunk, a dead ringer for the model Fabio whose image has graced the covers of many romance novels.

Maybe he is Fabio.

She is far from being his equal in the looks department. Chubby and plain of face tending towards downright homely.

And he loves her deeply.

They've come from some kind of event that looks at least semi-formal. He is wearing a ruffled shirt reminiscent of a Vegas lounge singer, and she is dressed in some sort of a gown.

She is sleeping deeply against his massive chest and shoulder. He supports her head with one hand. At a certain point, she half wakes up and asks him something, and he gently strokes her hair and shushes her back to slumberland.

She means the world to him; that much is obvious.

There are several sleek New York City women in this car, two of them with exercise mats strapped to their backs.

They are clearly coming from or going to someplace where they will strengthen their cores. The looks of incomprehension and incredulity on their faces as they watch this couple are priceless.

MADELINE ARTENBERG

Guardians of the Good

I had a hundred unhappy men
under me, who never had a woman
boss, certainly not a slight girl.

Openers, Verifiers, Packers handled
incoming mail for U.S. Customs.
When I spoke, they cat-whistled
and wiggled their middle fingers
at me.

After the Floor Captain grabbed
a cache of videotapes off
conveyor belts, men jammed
into the projection room, examined
them for anything beyond missionary.

I heard their braying,
kept to my office, cataloging pornography
by violation and country of origin:
Denmark, Sweden, Holland.

When the Floor Captain burst
through my door, licking
his lips, he slapped
the day's haul of magazines on the desk,
took bets on my stammer and blush.

After a while, I slept
with one eye open
while America
rested easy.

SIMONE NIKKOLE AZÚCAR

Diamond Flower

if my diamond was a woman
she would flower as she said my name
she would spread her petals

1. I wish I could circumcise my lips to rid you of 5 years of torment, 5 years of sacrificial healing.

2. I hope you don't remember them.
I heard that we can finally reverse the trauma brain.

3. but where was that scientific advancement when you were 9.

4. when you are 12. 12 poems bled your pain. ink stains are still maintained on your heart.

5. I heard time heals all wounds. what happens when time reopens wounds with each guy that smiled my way.

6. I know I turned my back on you but I too have to heal from my pain. I don't clean myself like men so remnants of wolves in sheep's clothing still remain. no matter how many times I am showered in ochún waves and God's rays.

7. the sun doesn't visit here that often. clothes limit the progress of healing from this train wreck of a past. a past that was never supposed to be written like that.

8. so I guess that's why you picked up your pen. your fingers took a break from caressing me to try to be free of the weeds they left because they didn't know when to leave.

9. leave. leave. leaves. they blow in the breeze but their presence is never forgotten. when are you going to get that appointment to reverse the

damage. the grey matter. the white matter. all pain whatever color matters.

10. I wish I could circumcise my lips to exercise the demons who followed you and looked like love. But you would've never glowed like you do now. stamping your presence as healing in action. marking your eyes with hope. a defibrillator to your big heart.

10. 10. 10. your big heart beats again every time he reminds you of your magic. your beauty. and challenges your creativity. so, you bloom every so brightly. ever so strong.

STAN BAKER

Stay Woke

Greetings fellow members of the Coma Survivors Support Group. Or as I like to say, my "coma compadres." As you know, until just recently, I was in a coma for over a year so, as is the custom here, I'd like tell you what I've been doing since I woke up. Or as everyone's saying nowadays, since I "got woke." Heh, heh. Yeah. My memory skills are still pretty messed up, but nevertheless, I decided I'd try to get back into the profession of my youth, acting. Believe it or not, getting an agent was easy. They heard I'd been in a coma for a year and that was all they needed to know. And it gets better. I booked my *first* audition! And get this, I'm going to be in the new movie by… Woody Allen! It's a dream come true! And believe me, after a year in a coma, I know something about dreaming. So, I met Mr. Allen in his office which, for some reason, was filled with what looked like… nursery school furniture? Anyway, he asked me what I thought about his movie "Manhattan," the one where his character was in love with a schoolgirl. I had to admit I had not seen it. And that was it! I got the part! So, then he drops the biggest news of all. I'm going to be co-starring with none other than… the great Louie C.K.! God, that man is so funny. And so sensitive. It seems like he really respects people. Especially women. It's like, to him, women are goddesses and he'd be happy to just stand there, and… admire them. But what do I know? I've been in a coma for a year. Anyway, the rest of the cast is amazing, too. Casey Affleck! He plays a sleepwalker who winds up in other people's bedrooms not knowing how he got there. And Jeffrey Tambor, from "Transparent," plays his mother. That guy really knows how to play women. Right? Oh boy. And there's going to be cameos by major personalities like Matt Lauer, Charlie Rose, and Garrison Keillor. You'd think those guys would be too busy, but I guess everyone wants to work with Woody. Oh, and I met the producer, Harvey Weinstein. He seemed kind of… bummed out. And I'm not sure why he was wearing a bathrobe. Anyway, then, in walks my favorite actor of all time, Kevin Spacey! He's playing the lead! I'm so stunned I blurt out, "Somebody pinch me." And believe it or not, Kevin *did*! Not a mean pinch, like his character on "House of Cards." Just a nice friendly pinch. On my tushie. I think they're all in a club and a butt pinch is their secret handshake. Anyway, I've got to go now. I haven't told my family about this yet and I can't wait to see the look on their faces when I share the good news with my wife and my three teenage daughters. They're going to flip out! So, in closing, my fellow members, I wish you all the best of luck, and as they say, "Stay woke."

BURTON BAROFF

It's Good to Know

"To know" is not one + one is two,
I know + I know is not always "I know."
I sort of know of a fifth season,
bundled by unrelenting time,
careening away, it's hard to keep pace,
so many breaths in every step.
I know I haven't tossed in the towel,
I just need shorter three-minute rounds,
I know the numbers of oft-time callers,
I know we humans bud and bloom but once.
Reluctantly the flower wilts,
inevitably the fragrance fades,
I know we nurture niggardly,
truly this perplexes me.
I know a plate filled with me, leaves me empty,
A plate filled with you nourishes my soul
Paradoxically speaking, "To Know"
is ego, all aglitter in off key notes,
"To know" is as well, knowledge, singing unadorned.

AMY BARONE

Message

She hovered outside my bedroom window
one late steamy morning in July.
I barely recognized her with wings spinning,
nose prodding,

as I pondered whether to begin the day.
But she vanished and my mind drifted further.
Until August when she returned,
singing from her bright blue throat as if an urgency awaited.

My mother relished nature's dance from this window.
She saved news clippings of successful writers for my visits.
A petite sugar-lover who fiercely guarded her nest. Loved music.
Revisited to relay a message I continue to decode.

KEVIN BECKER

Butte's Heroes

It was 1920 in old Butte, Montana
The mining was booming through picks and bandanas
Everybody prospered from hills full of copper
Well dressed, restaurants, and evenings full of opera
But by 1940 their ore had diminished
So, they ripped off the lid of their mountain to finish
Thus, they created "The Berkeley Pit"
Where precious metals were stripped with efficiency and wit
But they couldn't keep up with the price ever falling
On the turquoise colors they all thought enthralling
Forty years later on Earth Day '82
The mine was abandoned and pumps shut down too
As nature would have it, the groundwater leaked
Into the hole of a mountain where it's soul once was reaped
Filling a mile wide and two thousand feet deep
A lake full of acid from the pyrite beneath
A toxic disaster that keeps rising faster
To reach the groundwater and rivers that scatter
The laughter has ceased as scientists chattered
After solutions to rebuke the matter
Meanwhile through clouds of loud thunder
A flock of geese land on the lake to take cover
Drinking a draught, they thought would bring life
Killed every last one on that dark stormy night
Some people wept, pointed their fingers and blamed
For the monstrous disaster they let out his cage
Until something peculiar washed up from the storm
A slimy green substance three inches long
They started to study. Behold it's alive!
Life in deaths clutches, where nothing survives
These little green sponges were scrubbing the lake
Erasing the poison away from the place
Making the water a drink you could taste

My thoughts are now thinking this was no mistake
The micro avengers were actually yeast
Found deep in the bodies of a few little geese

LUCIANN BERRIOS

To Life

And my insides spill out
Through eyes glazed over
At memories of loving, of losses,
Of all the friends and lovers who came and went
Both sadness and joy in each swell, in each quiet outpour
Moved to tears by the fires put out,
By the passions ignited, by the movement of lives lived
At heartbreaks I try to soothe for dear friends
The very kind I am susceptible to
At rekindled teenage lovers, finding each other after all these years
Still attached by the strings the heart could not sever
My insides spill out, for the perfect vision
That hindsight provides, like a gift that kisses you
With calm and calamity
The beauty and duality of life
These truths upon truths, eyes more open
Heart meeting it wider, fuller
Yet more room to receive
Life beautiful highs, its suffocating lows
All of us just doing our best
Let us leave or greet each other in love
Let us all see more presently the future
With acceptance and gratitude
The sun hates not the cloud for its rain
Knowing it's time to shine comes as it always does
Clouds must rain and he must shine
For together both darkness and damp, coming before and after light
Nurtured flowers to grow
Us and flowers
Love and loss, high and low
My insides spill out to life
This affliction to hold onto what I can't control
To moments already in the process of passing

To things, to people, to myself as I know it
Change is the only thing we can be sure of
For home is wherever your voice is
How attached we get to the places that hold the most memories
As if without those four walls they'd be
Gone

PETER BLAXILL

Words from Underneath

You up there
we cannot see you lay your wreaths
see your tears
but do not grieve for us
We are having dances in the earth
holding talks with slugs
invited to dine with the Queen of Ants
calling *hi-ho* to passing worms
while our coffins rot   their silks decay

You up there
away
with black armbands   black veils
psalms   prayers
Go party
Go laugh in white suits and red dresses

You up there
we toast you
Guess what we're having for dinner
dust
delicious
Come on down
Don't be shy
You've got a map
Yes, the route will be rough
but never fear
you'll find your way
sometime or other

CREIGHTON BLINN

Monday Evening, East 14th Street, around 10:00

The used ice
Tumbles into plastic bins,
Clinking like the discarded glasses
Swept up by the server,
As she deftly avoids the bassist
Poised just a little too far from
The singer bravely
Competing with the din
Of conversations bouncing against each other,
Connections made, strengthened, abandoned,
Dialogues winding down another Monday
Mixed from equal parts yelp & yawn
And stirred into that perpetual tease
Of this being the one,
Where everything finally
Falls into place.

BERNARD BLOCK

Jeru

for Gerry Mulligan/Chet Baker/Stan Getz
(after Jeru's repertoire)

Bernie's tune   lullaby of leaves
doing the carioca   on the line for lions
soft   walking shoes   O dear *Jeru*
pass through the turnstile   I may be wrong but

Take the freeway
turn left at   night at the turntable
carioca   frenesi   makin' whoopee
five brothers   festive minor   lullaby of leaves

O *Jeru*   bark for barksdale   aren't you
glad you're you   bathing in
moonlight in Vermont   beginning to see
the light   my old flame   utter chaos

My funny valentine   little willie leaps
moves   whispering   come out
wherever you are   what's new   you say   the
soft shoe   crazy rhythm   half nelson

All the things you are   and aren't
festive minor   darn that dream
gone with the wind
lullaby of leaves

DIANE BLOCK

The Window

Do you remember Mama every morning how
we stood at the picture window in the living room
still as trees   you and I
   no word spoken
   peering out and peering in

Every morning   summer autumn winter spring
upon waking (still sleepy-eyed)   before
breakfast   before walking to school or doing chores
we stood   you and I
silent as the winter snow on the window pane

And do you remember one Christmas long ago
Father painted the Holy Mother and Child upon
that picture window   from the sofa in
the living room on a December morning I
watched him as he painted   slow and steady   then

drifted asleep in the hush   Come
twilight when I awoke Father was still painting
The next day the sun shone through
the blue red green gold   a prism
of color in a living room a-glow

Do you know Mama dear fifty years later
your daughter stands at her own window
every morning   summer autumn winter spring
Upon waking (still sleepy-eyed)   before
breakfast she stands at the window in the kitchen
   no word spoken   peering out…and peering in

BARBARA ANN BRANCA

Declination

She declined
>He asked her twelve times

She declined every time
>He was just a waning moon

She was a winter sun
>Rays wan, not wanton

She was all angles heard on high
>Eyes at odds with that mouth, that mouth

She spoke thunder
>Silver tongue slicing
>Sliver moon

After solstice
>His soul stitched

To try anew
>They must wait till
>Equinox

EVE BRANDSTEIN

Start of the Blues

It can start by reading the headlines or
hearing the radio highlights
or the editorial
or the gossip column
sometimes it's not the news at all
it's a phone call from another city
from an email
an Instagram
Facebook post
another time in my life
history kept tucked away
trees turn grey
above the sky waste and warning
illegal acts everywhere
untold deaths by normal people who say it's normal
to exterminate what's in the way
or crush the memory of it all
sometimes Charlie Parker
sometimes Sylvia Plath
sometimes suicide without a stanza or a verse
a personal choice
giving up with so much life
my own appetite for satisfaction
when disappointment meets the craving
with a sigh so deep
it crosses the line begins
to taste like salt
It can start because of a bad noise
or a broken nail
a bad conversation

about what didn't happen
when I tried & tried
sometimes I see someone I think is better

Rimes of The Ancient Mariner

sometimes I hear Blue Moon

sometimes it's just the way the sun sets
or the way the night arrests my eyes
or the scent of jasmine & sweat
or the crunch of leaves
the crackle of the fire
sometimes it's the rain
and sometimes…
sometimes it's just your name

DENVER BUTSON

In Which You Were Homesick

in which you were homesick for a time when it was still possible to
get lost in which if we have learned anything we haven't learned it
from this phrasebook in which there were horses running through
the sunlight as if we didn't have a choice to not believe in beauty in
which you were dreaming of things falling and when you woke up
there were things falling in which a man who looked like he slept
in an ashtray paced back and forth on the corner with a smoking
briefcase laughing and shaking his head and then put the briefcase
down and walked away while it drizzled confetti even though there
was no parade in which there was a cellist at your breakfast table
and she was lovely and you were twenty-one and you have no idea
what ever happened to her in which you were sleeping and then
you woke up and there was suddenly Chicago through the
windshield in which your father was dying and decided to fall out
of an airplane and you were certain that he would do something to
make sure that his chute didn't open but it did and he stood up and
started telling jokes all over again as if he hadn't just fallen through
the clouds in which you swim and you swim and you swim and
you still don't know if you really know how to swim in which a line
of people is walking toward the horizon and some people are
joining the line without knowing why and one of them says *even if
we get to that horizon there will be another one farther out what
then?* in which you had been making out for so long in someone's
basement that your tongue hurt and you thought your jeans might be
warn smooth at the crotch in which the conductor of this train
dreams of becoming an astronaut and is quite sure that his wife is
having an affair with his sister in which the ocean is always the
ocean even if we act as if there is no ocean out there in which there
is an abandoned house just off the highway and there is a windmill
next to the house and after you climb over the barbed-wire fence
and walk around the cow patties and step then through what was
once the front door of that house you announce *honey I'm home* and
you feel like you are indeed home perhaps for the first time in a

very long time in which there are dishwashers dreaming of becoming poets and poets washing last night's dishes and the same cardinal is outside both of their windows in the morning singing *am I alive am I alive am I alive?* in which here continues the long slow lesson of the loneliness that seems to have no beginning that seems to have no end

MICHELE CARLO

My Fiery NYC

They, the faceless ones, say if you play with fire you will get burned. But I beg to differ because I've played with fire my entire life and suffered not even one singed hair. Because I'm a native New Yorker. And no matter how long you've lived here, no matter how much of a New Yorker you think you've become, you'll never know the New York I know...

...the real New York: with junkies and bums and drunks; graffiti and garbage and punks. I mean real punks. Not those pseudo-skinhead tribal-tattooed trustafarians slumming from Connecticut. I mean *real* punks. Like Joey Ramone. He was from Forest Hills. And if you knew what growing up in what *you* would call a small town but *we* call a hood could do to you... you'd know why New York is the birthplace of both hip-hop... and punk!

The New York I know is a whirling incendiary creative supernova that fueled Walt Whitman, Marianne Moore, Nora Ephron, Spike Lee, Betty Smith, Piri Thomas, Lou Reed, Laura Nyro, Notorious B.I.G... and thousands of others both famous and infamous. The New York I know had nok-hockey, skully and manhunt, Brentano's bookstore, Unique Clothing Warehouse and Azuma, Dr. Pepper concerts, Tad's Steaks, Orange Julius, Theater 80...and real live artists living in Soho.

In my New York we used to cut class and ride the subway down to Greenwich Village—it was like the Highlander back then, there was only one—and we'd sit on someone's stoop with our Newport Lights and our R.C. Cola and pray for a tourist to ask us for directions just so we could say, "Fuck you!"

In my New York, kids wore the proud scars of playground battles: lumpy foreheads, scabby knees, missing fingers—hey, there was no padding under the monkey bars back then. But there were broken Rheingold bottles. No, not the trendy microbrew sipped by goateed hipsters, but the scuzzy swill guzzled by old men with no teeth who would die soon.

Yeah, there were broken bottles and used needles, and if you fell off a swing and broke something, hey it was your fault! Cause you were a pussy, a momma's child, a douchebag with sweaty palms and no heart whose momma made you wear skips. And who were you gonna sue anyway? No one's father wore a suit to work, those were only for funerals and if he wore one otherwise? Then he was a douchebag, too.

There were no cell phones in my New York. Your moms threw you out of the house at 8:30 in the morning and you came back when you got there. "It's 10 p.m., do you know where your children are?"

The hell you do! Because they're at Orchard Beach, they're at Coney Island, they're in a parking lot at the Bronx River projects watching a skinny-ass kid with a boom box under a streetlight who doesn't yet know he is going to be Grandmaster Flash.

In my New York, seven kids would share a soda, eight a piece of gum; we called it "ABC: Already Been Chewed" and if you dropped it, you kissed it up to God and stuck it right back in your mouth. No one ever got sick. What was sick? Sick was what happened to your grandmother who threw her slippers at you because she caught you stealing her Bacardi 151. Again.

Sick was what they tried to make you when they sent you to your cousin's house when they all had German Measles and they told you to get in the bed with them. But you never got sick. You had a cold beer on a hot summer's day, a second plate of roast perñil with tostones if you were hungry and you finished your meal with a café con leche and a cigarette, and if you happened to be seven months pregnant at the time...so the fuck what!

Speaking of coffee, there was no Starbucks, ice coffee was what happened when you left your cup on the fire escape. Times Square was a place you stayed away from. Bad neighborhoods were bad neighborhoods: there was no Park Slope *South* or Williamsburg *East* or Harlem *Heights*. The "D" in Avenue D stood for death—and drugs. Now you spend $300 on weed and think you scored. In the New York I knew, you got 10 joints to a dime bag, yeah, that's right, *ten* and if you didn't, you'd go right back and call the dealer a fucking retard. Except you can't say "retard" anymore. And that is what New York has become: a place where you can't eat a cheeseburger if you're pregnant, kids are prisoners in their own homes and a fucking ice coffee costs five fucking bucks. Do I sound bitter? I don't mean to…I'm actually hopeful.

Because I was forged in New York City fire. When phones were in the kitchen and water came from faucets. Where a tree grew in Brooklyn, a rose in Spanish Harlem and Rosie is still and always will be The Queen of Corona. And no matter how much they, the faceless ones, try to suck out all the oxygen and drain off all the piss and vomit; no matter how much high-tech foam they try to pump over us, the raging, creative, eternal fire that is New York City: the fire that some of us risked our lives for and others have died for—will never, ever die. For in that fire is freedom. The freedom to ignite anything your mind can spark…and go wherever the smoke and embers take you.

I know. I've lived my entire life on the lip of the volcano and survived to tell you about it. Because I'm from New York City. Where every night is Saturday night. The party starts when I get there. Now get the fuck out of my way!

PATRICIA CARRAGON

Reach Out for the Moment

I look into the water's eyes,
see your face
where mine ought to be.
It rises to the surface,
diverts me from a future
hidden in uncertainty.

Your kindness mesmerizes—
my tears, welcomed guests.
Your voice rises from the water,
tears this veil spun from sadness.

You speak of life after death,
of mending a damaged spirit,
of how innocence erases time
from the hourglass of life,
of a world reborn
in love and freedom,
untouched by history's impact
where sorrow rose from smoke.

I watch the smoke fade
as light cuts its veil.
Together,
we leave history
by the harbor doorstep.
We reach out for the moment,
touch in light's seduction.
We rise as one entity,
we resurrect as love.

MARIA CHISOLM

For Langston Hughes

In the house of Mr. Hughes
where he sat and slept and prayed
In the house of Mr. Hughes
where he ate and wrote for days
House of language
cups of tea
booshie black folks
novelist was he

Sleepless nights in the house of Hughes
where he ate and wrote for days
books and language was his thirst
lit up the house in praise

PAT CHRISTIANO

For the Poet Who Stopped Screaming One Day
for Iris Berman

This is for the poet who ran out of ammo
this is for the poet who ran out of words
and started screaming one day
this is for the poet who stopped screaming
because who listens anyway
or maybe just stopped
to listen for a moment
this is for the silent poet

this is for the poet disappointed
in life or in love or in anything
to the point of disappearing
but returns

this is also for the artist
also the musician
for the cook and the dancer
the social worker the beautician

this is for the poet who returns
to his world and his words
reassembles them carefully
completely alone
this is for the poet alone
who rehearses his craft
and rehearses his craft
and rehearses his craft
for why not say
nothing
And this is a picture of the poet
on the back of her book
the one that was published

to a sort of mild interest
and to her own surprise
she is standing in sunlight
on the roof of her building
the one she didn't jump from

DEBORAH CLAPP

Reflection

I remember the night of moments with you
Together we lived these moments in moments
Where no time lives at all
Where there is only the clearest, round reflection
Circle of light, oneness of being, luminous knowing
Where the full bloom in the delicate bud knows the secret of every petal's
unfolding
Where the prince in the frog knows my kisses in the small rocks, I throw
Where the mother in the man in the moon knows us as
The child needing to know
You said, "Look!" pointing up to the moon
I looked up and saw pale yellow covered by gray cloud
It radiated up and out
Suddenly, the gray cloud started moving diagonally down to the left
It quickly unveiled the clearest round reflection
(Circle of light, oneness of being, luminous knowing!)
"Look!" I cried, "She's saying 'Hello!'"
Together we watched the revelation of the moon
A ceremony of recognition, just for us
When she was all revealed, you said
"It's nice to receive a telegram from way out in space"
I smiled, knowing your heart… Stop
As we walked to the Path together, I said, "We can remember that"
You said, "I already do!"

LORRAINE LOFRESE CONLIN

Streets of Innocence

As a child, I saw
things next door as different.
The kids had no Mom or Dad
wore ragged clothes and
were often home alone.

Their grandmother never greeted them
with a kiss or hug when she came home
she'd grab the boy Kippy by his ear,
often smacked his head asking why
he didn't do something or other,
yet paid no attention to his sister Saundra
allowed her to stay out with me
until a parent called me in.

With a smile and a piece of old clothesline
Saundra made new friends,
showed us how to skip rope
how fast to turn and
sing silly rhymes as we jumped.

She said little but
what she did say warned,
not paying attention
could get *yawl* a whip across the shins
hard enough to send you to your knees.

Seeing what looked like burn scars
on her brown skin, we heeded her words,
in awe of how Saundra could out-jump,
out-last every turn.

I can still hear sounds of soles

skidding on pavement,
the songs sung breathlessly
the slap of rope coming
'round and 'round.

WILLIAM CONSIDINE

Dark Party

Poem begins after the dark party.
The beer in the tub poured cold as nails.
Strangers smirked in my barren study.
The music of my dance blasted the guests

To huddle in the far, dim kitchen, cold.
A chilly guest lit the oven, door open.
Neighbors spoke boldly of my shock and
Trauma. A stud-skirted woman smiled

Behind the cold friend I could not see
To the door. Some of the guests stayed
In their tiny homes and did not show
Their fear and confusion. Tight-lipped,

I paced my railroad hall. This is fun,
Drinking friends demanded. I'll throw another
Soon and a strange word will go round and round
And round: call it a success, just do it.

STEVE DALACHINSKY

Afterglow

the sun's afterglow stretches across the river like a body surfer
the river a constantly moving body disperses the light
across its rippling skin
the sun creates as much light as it does shadow
the light thins as night's shadow stretches across the river
the river no longer impresses the runners
the runners no longer run by the river's edge
clouds obscure day's end
obscure are the no longer panting dogs
the pre-ancient bard conducting the river's currents
currently it is that time after the world has ended
& her smile as she passes does not seem like a blind woman's smile
i sit on a bench made of steel & wood
after the world as we know it has come to an end
as the afterglow fades with her face into evening
& her smile & this bench & the big red **W** on the other side
of the river   no longer exist
& the Queen of Hearts & all the other party boats no longer exist
& the highway behind me that often would sound like an ocean
has fallen silent as i have   for it & i
no longer exist

but of all the passersby i've seen & i've seen a lot
before the world as we knew it came to an end
that smile on a stranger's lips endured
& i almost could have endured the end of the world because of that smile & the now
faded afterglow
but my memory ended when i did & i ended when the world did
along with so much else
& now not even an umbrellas no longer openly catch the rain
nor will the morning's greenery fetch even a grin.

ANGELA DiCAMILLO

Suds

To kiss his cold lips
That just yesterday,
Felt so warm on hers.

He loved her.
Does he still love her,
Where he is now?

She scrubs his blood from the sidewalk,
Mixing memories with
Warm sudsy water.

BANG!
"Sorry, ma'am we did all we could."

Smiles, lingering looks,
Cheap circlets of gold.
Can she recall love with so little?

Today she'll scrub, tomorrow,
They'll walk over what's left of him.
Children will try to find blood in the cement
A game!

She wasn't the first to scrub
Her life from the sidewalk.
She won't be the last.

MELIORA DOCKERY

The Recalcitrant Child

The bench in the front porch feels hard and cold and the chipped paint of the latticework, where roses climb in the summer, stands out in a supernatural blue. At nine years old I know I'm in trouble. I've missed the first bus to school and I'm in danger of missing the second but I feel rooted to the spot. I just want to sit here for 100 years and never move.

It's a Tuesday. It's always bacon and eggs on a Tuesday – my favorite. Oh the joyful smell of bacon and eggs wafting up to the room that I share with my older sister. But I'm not hungry. I'm never hungry these days.

My mother, edgy and nervous over my behavior, has packed me up in my winter coat, my beret, my gloves and my satchel strung across my shoulder. But once out in that porch I can't move on.

I just sit there. I don't even know why I just sit there. I don't even know why I'm not hungry. My mother is a fabulous cook, eclectic in her choices, cooking vegetarian dishes she learnt from her mother, the anti-vivisectionist – nut cutlets with a tomato sauce, flaky vegetable pie. But lately, I take one bite and food just seems stuck in my throat. My mother has variously cajoled, remonstrated, hugged, chastised but that darn food just gets stuck every time.

Eventually, the front door opens and my mother comes out, horrified to see me still sitting there. She drags me back in and divests me of my satchel, still strung across my chest, my coat, my beret and I stand disconsolately staring at my reflection in the bright shine of the dining room table, watching as she cleans the ashes out of the grate. Neither of us knows what to say. Little clouds of ash rise with each beat of the brush and finally she mutters, more to herself than to me, "I've tried everything. I've cooked her favorites, I've asked what's wrong, I've given extra love, I've remonstrated. I don't know what else to do." And then to my horror she turns, "I'm going to starve you. That's what I'm going to do. No more food. You're cut off."

I think of the starving Chinese children: Those children who I've been told deserve my uneaten food. Those children who I imagine have been receiving my leftovers, neatly packaged in a brown paper parcel and tied with string like

Christmas. The parcel sailing over the ocean for months so that by the time they open it, eager and excited, there is nothing but disappointment and a moldy lump of nut cutlet. Will I start receiving stale noodles and rotted bok choy from all those children who are returning the favor?

I do not want to be one of the starving children. I regain my appetite, and to my regret, I have never lost again it to this day.

GABRIEL DON

Reluctant Relationship

It was the summer of discontent when I reluctantly entered a relationship and the cherry trees had stopped vibrating like a love song to the sun, the flowers had bloomed and burnt out. The streets were full of people seeking the shady side of the road, ice cream trucks sang proudly parked at schools. Lust is a giddy trickster. Operated by (what I called terrible) this netherworld and deprived of (what I called happiness) stability; I sought the assistance of a doctor. His name was Steve Smith or so the gold lettering on his door declared. Suspiciously, I eyed his name from the squashy scratchy chair in his waiting room and decided to question everything he told me—at least internally.

Therapeutic talk was not something I had ever paid for before. This duty was usually undertaken by Cassandra, an emotional soundboard, my oldest dearest friend. But infatuation and desire for her man (who I referred to as a boy) caused her to ignore me. Calling her in an attempt to be cured of my desire for a boy with big shoes, I found that Cassie was no longer at my best-friend-beck-and-call. She too had found a significant other to enter (what I referred to as inertia and torture) a relationship with. Every time I called, she was on her way to class or at work yet somehow she was always drinking or eating cheap Thai, dancing to Dixieland Ragtime jazz—breaking my heart with her Facebook and Instagram photos. I really needed to speak to her but my texts informing her I was terrified went unanswered.

The symptoms had appeared so suddenly, like how quickly the door closes with your keys on the inside, like the flip of a switch, toast butter side down on the floor, I became completely addicted to Harry. All I wanted was to be kissed or hugged by him, vibrating at his touch, shaking when he appeared, walking towards me smiling on the street or standing at my front door, dimples divine. Around the same time, I started feeling this way, I had started taking birth control pills and thought it could be my hormones all jacked up so I stopped taking them but I still didn't feel any better. "Where are you going?" we'd ask each other when the other was going to the bathroom. That's how bad it had gotten.

So, I made an appointment with a psychiatrist (Steve Smith. Google Search). He wasn't actually the first person I saw about my issue. I had seen a Dr. Brenden Kowalski (far less skeptical about his name) one week prior to Dr. Smith. Dr. Kowalski—the doctor title perhaps unearned unless you consider psychiatrists to be doctors, counseling a medicine—laughed at me. When I told him, I'm considering ending my relationship and it's the last thing I'd ever want to do but it was making me sick, he made me feel stupid and silly. Mostly he was just uninterested. Old men rarely take notice of what young females have to say.

Before I met Harry, I preferred masturbation to sex. He touched me better than I touched myself. Far gentler. At work over the photocopy machine, sweating in my grey high-waisted skirt and collared white shirt with three-quarter sleeves, perspiring, glowing, my mind tossed around, *Sex with Harry, Sex with Harry, Sex with Harry.* We did it on the washing machine with a shoe inside (extra vibrations) and masturbated in his office as he counted the till after closing the bar until he gave up on numbers and money. Needing someone other than yourself is the worst feeling. Love makes a lunatic out of reasonable people. I called Cassie constantly but she never had any free time to talk to me. My mother was very skeptical when I told her I was seeking therapy and sighed into the receiver, "I hope it helps, darling but please be cautious."

Would I, fiddling with my nails, peeling them down too close to my fingers, tell the doctor about when I lived with my aunt, twelve years old at the time and no sense of sexuality (though some of my friends had developed one: telling me terrifying tales of how their neighbor-boyfriend played with their pubic hair) my aunt cornered me in the pantry to let me know she had her eyes on me. Her perfectly made-up face invigorated with jealous insecurity and hate, "You stay away from my husband." To know then what one knows now isn't always beneficial. Innocence a haven. I didn't know what she meant.

The implications of this statement came to me far later in life. On my 21st birthday, I watched my philandering uncle, balding and big-bellied, flirt with my friends and listened to the disdainful comments of my sinewy aunt directed at the younger females. "A minute on the lips forever on the hips," she said to Cassie who was enjoying my white chocolate mud cake. Moist wet slippery vanilla sponge layered with buttery mousse and cased in hard sweet coco-less-chocolate-casing amusing our mouths. "When I was your age women paid attention to what they ate," she eyed the cake on our plates and continued with a downward glance at Cassie's blossoming breasts, "Though you look great with more weight on you." Shifting on her pointed elbow she turned her address to me, "You're so tall, Raquel." I hate women who hate women.

Filling out basic information form, sitting in Smith's more comfortable office chair, far sleeker than the waiting room fabric. Insurance details. Personality tests. On a scale of one to five: Do you feel depressed? 1. Rarely -- 5. Very Frequently. (Circled five).

"They are a stranger so they are impartial," I told my mother, in defense of my choice. "Everyone has an agenda," my mother said. "I wish you'd stop choosing the path of most resistance," she continued. I could see her head shaking at my relationship over the receiver. It wasn't a choice! I was in love. Love is not alchemy: it is fossilization. It turns gold to coal. Love is a remote, in the hands of another, which controlled my barometer of happiness. The temperature moves up and down the thermometer according to their mood, not only my own, anymore. Love is a shove above my stomach, when the pressure is released, when love is over (inevitable: have you met me?) it leaves a hole. Love is a focus point, from which forward motion becomes not possible.

People always blame a woman's father for her relationship issues. I have a fantastic father and I still have issues. If anything, I have mother issues. I seek to be *mothered*, looked after and at the same time my independence doesn't allow me to let others do so, independence not always a positive quality. My poor mother, trying to tend to me as a little girl, my despondent, "I CAN DO IT MYSELF." When I was a little child if I got hurt or scared, a bump to the knee, a yell in my ear, I would hold my breath and stop breathing until I turned the wrong shade. This worried my mother so much she took me to a doctor who calmed her down, "She'll eventually pass out and once she faints, her body will naturally return to regular breathing patterns."

My mother likes to remind me, "Chickenpox was no big deal for you, just for me." Having never naturally caught it as a child or teenager, her parents never making her visit a sick neighbor so immunities kick in youth, my mother fell very ill, as adults do with the disease, pox inside her throat and womb. Infection in adults tends to be more severe. "I was very sick and looked like a monster." Reminders as we went through family photos, ones of us as a unit when negatives were still developed, calamine lotion white polka dots upon us all. We were an itchy twosome.

Cassie's parents were extremely Catholic and no matter how much she denied her Catholicism it had touched her as all Catholics remain touched. She had nineteen siblings. No joke. Every sperm is sacred was taken literally and with birth control out of the question and abstinence the only solution to remain without child for two warm-bodied humans her brothers and sisters popped out like corn kernels in a hot pot. Most of her brothers joined the navy or became doctors. After many summer camps themed with Jesus, they thought they ought to.

Because Cassie was beautiful, Cassie was cursed. Every boy in school had apparently slept with her. Their fathers too. No one was safe. The day the high school board announced a minimum length on our dowdy grey uniform skirts, she came with it cut so high we could see what we later called her cunt. Her short as short, short shaded skirt over her sweaty thighs, legs spread (never *lady-like*) as we ate two-dollar tacos and sipped 99 cent corn syrup saturated iced tea. "How old are you again honey? Wait until you're my age," my aunt would warn us.

Our bodies were an endless source of pain and frustration. Once Cassie and I signed a treaty to only eat apples for a week while at the same time completing vigorous exercise routines. Running, Sit-ups. Sequences of silly things I can only, regrettably, describe as Butt-Ups. Scheduled starvation and sportsmanship every school morning. Harping on hipbones and rib cages we hated our Femininity as it kicked in with pheromones, fertility, and fuller figures. At school, I was always described as the second most beautiful girl in our class. Cassie obviously the first. I wish I could go back and tell us, we would never be so young again: so firm; unadulterated: un-aged; steady strong bodies; nipples, on unsagging breasts, pointing to the stars.

When Cassie and I were nineteen we had a moment of nostalgia for our teenage years, which we retracted faster than a bastard metal tape measurer (always cutting me on recall) when we spent too much time with her younger clan of brothers and their pubescent friends. They all had crushes on us and made it clear by constantly insulting us. Love demonstrated with negative attention. Invading a room Cassie had all to her own, despite her enormous amount of siblings. Taunting us on the trampoline we jumped on with dish soap, slippery suds. The boys, her brothers and their buddies, would stand anywhere they could to watch us bounce in our bikinis. Bodies not knowing which way was up or down.

"Mr. Smith, with all due respect this is serious. Please don't smile." A smile that sneered little *girl* you got the blues sarcastically. As if I'd never paid taxes or lost a parking spot. As if worrying wasn't for women. As if work wasn't for women. I had worked all the days of my life. Every day I worked in the unpaid, unappreciated position titled Woman.

"You're after my objective opinion?" Dr. Smith asked.
Dr. Smith handed me the sought-after tester packet of Pristiq and began to write on his prescription pad. I read the purple print pausing at *This medicine can increase thoughts of suicide* and cause the docent to *start to act reckless* warnings. The folded paper within the Pristiq packaging told me to call my doctor right away if I noticed any of these side effects:

1. Fast, pounding or uneven heartbeat
2. Seeing or hearing or feeling things that are not there
3. Swelling or tingling

66

4. Chest tightness, trouble breathing
5. Blurred vision
6. Chest pain, shortness of breath
7. Confusion, weakness, twitching
8. Feeling more excited or energetic than usual
9. Fever or chills
10. Numbness, tingling, or burning pain in your hands, arms, legs, or feet.
11. Seeing, hearing, or feeling things that are not there
12. Seizures or tremors
13. Unusual behavior or thoughts of hurting yourself or others
14. Unusual bleeding or bruising
15. Dizziness
16. Unusual dreams
17. Warmth or redness in your face, neck, arms, or upper chest
18. Ringing in your ears

This pharmacist had clearly never been in love.

SAARA DUTTON

Daddy's Girl

I am beautiful.

I know this because Daddy says I'm beautiful. He should. He created me to his own specifications; a combination of body parts from all the women in beauty pageants he's judged and owned, all the women he's fucked and owned.

Daddy is rich.

Though not quite as rich as people think. All that glitters is not gold, right? Sometimes it's gold plated or smudged brass. But he invested in me. Daddy bought me a new nose and a chin. My chin used to be like his. That is, I didn't have one. I always delete old photos of myself. I hate that you can see his face in mine, just under the surface. I am my father's daughter, but I don't like the resemblance.

Daddy bought me brand new tits and teeth too. My tits are huge. So are my teeth. Huge and white and it's a struggle to pull my lips over them as I speak in modulated tones. Did you know that my voice is what female robots are designed to sound like? It's true. I practiced my voice for hours and hours before trying it out on the public. It's a voice that says I'm in charge, but only if you agree. It's a GPS voice, reprogrammable at will.

Daddy loves me, this I know.

I am his favorite, though I don't take great pride in this. There isn't much competition. My little sister is weak and needy. My chinless brother married a dull woman with a double chin. Maybe she should give one of them to my brother.

Me, I married rich. Richer than Daddy.

Sure, I had to convert. But Daddy didn't mind. Money knows no religion. Marriage is a contract. So, I fulfilled my duty quickly and gave birth to two children in three years. A boy and a girl. Even though my babies bear my husband's name, Daddy knows I made them for him. He likes to be surrounded by his children and grandchildren, and I like to please him.

That's why I lost the baby weight within a month after both pregnancies. Daddy does not like fat women.

Every three weeks I get my roots touched up. Daddy likes blondes. My mother's hair is blonde, even now in her 60's. Of course, she hasn't been married to Daddy in 30 years. My daughter's hair is dull brown. But she is only six. One day it will be blonde too. Like the sun at a tropical resort. Like gold. Like chilled butter on a white tablecloth. Butter that remains untouched, because I don't eat the bread next to it. Blonde hair is powerful. So is the restraint it takes to not eat the bread. Power and wealth means having access to everything but refusing most of it.

Daddy likes powerful women. That's why he gave me the money to start my own fashion business. It wasn't a hard sell. He's always given me what I want: "Daddy, buy me a car! Daddy, I want to be a model! Daddy, I want to be fashion designer! Daddy, I want an office in the White House!" If I actually ate bread, I'd know which side it was buttered. So I design clothes he likes to see on women; form-fitting dresses and high heels. Women should look like women. Like the woman sign on a bathroom. She's in a dress for a reason. No one wants to enter the wrong door. There are rules.

The women who buy my clothes want my life. They mostly buy them on sale at ugly strip malls. They believe that buying my clothes is like buying a bit of my life. My clothes are tried on by hundreds of women; office workers, teachers, housewives. By the time a dress is purchased, it's covered in deodorant stains, lipstick smears, fingerprints, and strands of unwashed hair. I don't know these women, but they think they know me. They think I'm "classy", not knowing I'd never use that word. That's fine. That is my appeal. I know the power of keeping quiet. Silent like a mannequin in a department store, waiting to be dressed in this season's ideas. People project whatever they want onto me: I am sweet. I am wise. I am witty. I love children and working mothers and giving blowjobs.

People think I whisper sound advice to Daddy in private, although there's no evidence of this. My soft breath in his ear; a moral compass, his conscience, guiding him away from rash decisions and red buttons. Jiminy fucking Cricket with huge tits and teeth. It's a pretty picture. So, I don't need to provide proof of my good intentions. People need to believe in me, and that's enough.

What they don't know is that no one can reach Daddy. Have you ever really looked into his eyes? If you did, you'd understand. Yes, I know he loves me…in his own way. When people ask what I think about his sexist attitude, I don't know how to answer. He cannot change. He says sexual things about me and pats my ass because he only views women in one way. Like the sign on the bathroom. There is only one image: are you fuckable or not?

I am 36 years old. I am a year older than Daddy's expiration date for women. He is a businessman, and beauty is a useful commodity, like oil or cattle. It has value that diminishes year by year. Women my age are traded in for a younger model. So, I know he is cheating on my stepmother, who is six years older than me. I don't care about her. She's a gold-digging whore. But she's not stupid. She's a businesswoman too. She had to know this was coming, no matter how much yoga she does and trips to the plastic surgeon she makes. This was the deal she made.

The only part that bothers me is that Daddy is fucking my friend Faith.

It's funny that her name is Faith. Daddy was elected President on faith, not experience. Voters believed in him, in the power of our family name, hoping some luck would rub off on them like a cheap ring that turns your finger green. Now the faithful are getting fucked while Daddy is fucking Faith in the White House. It's comical. He never had any intention of helping them. He just liked hearing them shout his name. Just like my friend Faith. A sea of faithful voters, waiting to be told what to believe by a man who has no fixed beliefs.

But I don't care. That's their problem. You can't help people who are too stupid to leave their sad little towns with no jobs. There's no water in that well, no matter how thirsty you are. I'm not here to quench that thirst. It's not that I dislike them. I just don't think about them.

Not like my friend Faith.

I think about her a lot.

And I've started to hate her.

Faith is 10 years younger than me. She has 10 more years of currency than I do. She hasn't started looking for signs of aging in the mirror yet, examining the cosmetic tubes and jars, squinting at the fine print, rubbing fine lines, hoping for miracles, wondering when the power of beauty will diminish. When the value will decrease.

Fuck Faith.

Daddy used to look at me the way he looks at her. But not since I started having my husband's babies. Not since my value began to decline and my ass began to drop.

That's okay. I will win in the end. I have Daddy's name by birth. No one can take that from me. It's a power that Faith will never have. I am his brand. And one day when Daddy is dead, I will inherit the biggest chunk of his fortune. I have made sure of this. It is the only request I have actually whispered in his ear and made sure pen was put to paper.

One day I will stand by Daddy's coffin, grieving with elegance. Like Jackie Kennedy. I will not be hysterical. I will delicately dab my eyes with a pretty handkerchief. No snot will run out of my nose on onto my glossy lips. I will give the public what they want and no more. That's the deal. I will look beautiful in a black dress that I have designed. Cameras will flash. Sales will skyrocket.

And I will win. Just wait and see.

GIL FAGIANI

Night of The Hot Hoagie

Every night, chest out, face shiny,
Brigade Sergeant Samuel L. Silverman
bursts into my room
10 p.m., hunger hour
while I stand eyes forward,
gut in, shoulders back,
quivering like I have palsy.
Sergeant Silverman sniffs around
for a Philly-style hoagie sandwich:
cheese steak, shrimp salad,
hamburger, Italian.

He opens drawers
looks in coat pockets
lifts up blankets and sheets
when he finds a hoagie
confiscates half declaring: "R.H.I.P"
--Rank Has Its Privileges--
as the big knot in his throat
works itself up and down
and half my precious sandwich
disappears down his gullet.

Fed up with being ripped off,
I order an Italian flame-thrower
from Fran and Nan's Hoagie Shop:
prosciutto, salami, and provolone
all three layers larded with Tabasco,
Louisiana Hot Sauce,
and cherry peppers.

The next evening Sergeant Silverman
bursts into my room

picking up the scent of hoagie.
I make no attempt to hide it.
After the first few bites Sarge roars
and runs off to the latrine
where he latches his lips around
the cold-water faucet.

JASMINE FARRELL

Where I Come From

Well, now, Phoenix, where you from?

I come from Grandma's
New Year's Eve Rice N Peas,
stiff charismatic hair bangs
and
God-mommies who can sang, Baby.

I come from pride-
heroes, strength and a few lies

A lineage of stories that make the authors
of best sellers envious.
The older folk got tales, Baby.

Fierce Index finger to punctuate the line,
"I ain't gonna say it to you again verbally."

I come from passed down traditions
that should have remained
under vintage evening stars.

I come from hefty kisses,
Vaseline saturated lips.

I come from love

You know, that sweet sticky confusing peace
we always attempt to grab instead of receiving.

I come from love.

I come from cook-up rice, ackee and salt fish.
Pholourie, 4 for 1$ and ritualistic
Monopoly gamin' every other weekend
with aunty and uncle.

I come from playfulness.

Light hearted grins and cumbersome laughter
spilling over couches with the stench of mauby
and sorrel permeating Grandpa's living room.

I come from perseverance.

Hanging on to a thread
But,
Mama used the very hairs on her head
to make sure we remained hanging-
sometimes,
bending,
shaking, but,
never falling.
Never losing grip.

I come from grit.

The laced persistence
to place each foot in front of the other
in order to evolve.

Southern dialect, old wise tales
and old school routines.

Warm air, crisp bacon,
Tree swingin' in Valley Stream
scolding hot coffee,
Greasy Blue Magic scalp

and reflective pauses.

I come from *raised right*.
"Keep your elbows off the table,
Keep your head held high,
Keep your name clean,
And remember what your parents taught you."

I come from everything I needed
to get where I'm goin' to.

That's where I come from.

RICHARD FEIN

Drinking Buddies

From between parked cars he ran into the street,
one shoe on, one shoe off.
He was really trying but the drivers were alert.
His friend followed, dragged him back,
but he pushed away, ran, then parked himself
in a garbage can waist deep until
his friend gently raised him high
away from that dismal can.
Then he went almost limp,
and buried his face in his friend's dirty shirt.
He might have been sobbing.
But I had to go,
stay any longer and they'd curse at voyeur me,
or worse, I'd get involved.
But the next day I chose to walk
on that same skid row street.
There they were sitting on the same stoop,
two uprooted trees supporting each other,
arms like intertwined branches.
The friend had given him his shoe.
Two drinking buddies shoulder to shoulder,
one barefoot and the other with two left shoes.

DUANE FERGUSON

Sunrise, Sunset

Here I stand waiting for the tide to change.
Waiting for the sun to set.
Waiting for the day to end.
Waiting for the change that Sam said was comin'
That has me hummin I know… A change gon' come
Oh yes it is.

But what happens when change aint nuthin' but jangle in your pocket
And you still a dollar short of progress?

When marginalized bodies are still claimed and taxed and cashed on
Lining the banks of the elite like beached goliaths waiting to be stripped of
their worth?

Change aint nuthin' but a headline, a political ideology abandoned by the
so called oppressed
Clinging to a warped patriotism that turned weapons into righteous
symbols, flags into Gods and protests into calls of anarchy.

I know it took a while to get here. There have been many sunsets.
Sunsets filled with hope, progress and change.
Sunsets spilled with blood, calloused feet, broken batons and burnt bodies.

But with very sunset… the sun must rise again.

MARIPOSA MARIA TERESA FERNÁNDEZ

Sometime After Midnight

After Poetry Night at the Poets Passage
Old San Juan, 12/27/2017

Measures of suffering
Shall we compare?
         dark times bring full cups of
tears and fears / unseen wounds / anguish bared
by all the horrors of what dark times bring
and somehow, songbirds still sing

in these tropical skies of gloom
         dark clouds of doom

beyond the horizon, there
in the foreshadowing third eye of hurricanes
amidst ghosts and disaster-shocked minds
las pesadillas loom
in roofless rooms

dead weight / barely a hug / a coffin / a nail / a rock / bare soil, where
majestic trees cried out / screamed for survival
to live and grow laying down on the ground
or fell to their deaths
disoriented birds flew back home
to the shock and grief of losing their long-time nests
and then the vultures came

there is a measure to the pain one feels first hand
a bruise so deep / somatic shock waves travel far
and linger like radiation

losing endless nights
full of sorrow and no sleep
will never
    ever

compare yet
somehow equal
measures dig deep / so deep
in bottomless chasms of
el charco colonizado
that traumatically
join us all.

NICOLE FERRARO

Missing Mary

With the death of Mary Tyler Moore in 2017, the world lost an icon, and I put to rest a childhood dream.

As a woman born in the 80s, I came to Mary as a second-wave viewer. She appeared on my television for the first time when I was eight years old, courtesy of Nick at Nite rebroadcasting old sitcoms, like *I Love Lucy*, *Taxi*, and—best of all—*The Mary Tyler Moore Show*.

I remember sitting on the living room rug in my Care Bears nightgown, mesmerized when Mary first showed up on our screen. I loved her right away. I loved that her character Mary Richards was an independent woman. I loved that she had this great apartment and newsroom job, and that everyone adored her.

I couldn't get enough and soon started revolving my eight-year-old life around *The Mary Tyler Moore Show*. I tried to be home for all reruns. I stocked up on VHS tapes in the event of a "Marython." And I made my mom buy me multiple copies when TV Guide put out a commemorative issue celebrating Mary.

It wasn't just that I loved the show. I did and I do. But something about it and something about her made me feel at home at a time when I was struggling to find that comfort elsewhere.

Mary entered my life two years after my father died. Not only was his death a heartbreaking loss for me, but an isolating one. It made me feel separate from the kids at school who seemed so young to me now. It made me feel separate from my mom, who stopped talking about my dad after he died, so I did too. But I thought about him. And I thought about other bad things that might happen. But when Mary was on TV, things felt better.

So, it was only natural I became fixated on meeting her.

My first attempts were indirect, and embarrassing: like the day Aunt Donna was reading over my shoulder at Jones Beach to see what I was writing in my loose-leaf binder, and she howled aloud: "Dear Mr.

Asner?!" when she realized I was penning a fan letter to Ed Asner to see if he'd connect me and Mary.

I didn't send it.

But meeting Mary seemed like a possibility again a couple of years later when my grammar school P.S. 193 in Whitestone, Queens, got the Internet, and my fellow fourth graders and I were hooked up with our first email accounts on Prodigy.

We spent the first few weeks just emailing each other, figuring that's all this was for. But one afternoon, my computer teacher Mrs. A tapped me on the shoulder and handed me a slip of paper. It read: MTMary@prodigy.net

"Nicole," she said. "I have Mary Tyler Moore's email address… and I know how much you love her, why don't you send her a note and tell her what a big fan you are…?"

I was already typing before she could finish her sentence:

"Dear Mary, I'm 11 years old and your biggest fan. Thank you so much for The Mary Tyler Moore Show. I love it and I love you. Love, Nicole."

I looked up at Mrs. A, she looked down at me, we both nodded. And— *click*—I sent it.

I stayed up late that night, giddy and nervous, hoping I would get to school the next day and see a response. I knew it was a long shot, she probably wouldn't even read my email. But, for luck, I surrounded myself in bed with all the commemorative TV Guides.

The next morning, I ran straight to the computer lab, logged into my email account, waited… and waited. This was dial-up, so the waiting was at least three-quarters of the Internet experience.

Enough time passed, I was logged in. And there at the top of my otherwise empty inbox was this:

"Dear Nicole, thanks for your note, I'm so glad you love the show. Love always, Mary."

This was almost too much to handle. My jaw was open so wide it could have grazed the keyboard. My hands were shaking. I wanted to run through the halls. But I knew I needed to seize this moment to keep this going, so I hit reply:

"Dear Mary, Thanks so much for your response! Are you still friends with Rhoda and Mr. Grant?"

That night I went home and made the TV Guide bed shrine again. I arrived at the computer lab early the next day, and *bam*: "Hi Nicole - yes, I am still friends with Rhoda and Mr. Grant ☺"

Well, this was incredible. Over the next couple of weeks, I sent more casual notes telling her things about me, like "hey I'm the spelling bee champion again this week," and "I have a dance recital coming up," ordinary stuff like that.

But little did my computer teacher know when she orchestrated this friendship, is that there was one big reason I wanted to get to know Mary Tyler Moore.

In being obsessed with her, I had learned a lot of rough things about Mary's life—like the fact that she lost her son when he was in his 20s, and her brother and sister died as well. And since I already felt connected to her, I had this idea that Mary and I could help each other. Maybe she needed to talk to somebody about her loss, and I could talk to her about my dad.

I intended to bring this up over email, but I wanted to ease into it and wait until I felt we were close.

So about three weeks in, I went up to the computer lab, breathed in deep, and went for it:

"Mary," I wrote, "we've been friends a few weeks now… and I have to tell you, I know your son died, and I'm very sorry. I also wanted to tell you that my dad died, and if you need to talk to anybody about what you're feeling I am here, and I understand."

I hit send and exhaled.

Later that night, I stayed up again surrounded by the TV Guides, imagining what would come of this. Maybe Mary and I would go on Oprah together and weep with gratitude about how we saved each other from repressed grief.

But there was no response from Mary the next morning. And I never heard from her again.

At first, I was mortified. I knew it was wrong to talk to adults about this stuff. This was all my fault.

It wasn't until a year later that I discovered it was never Mary I was emailing with—it was just my computer teacher thinking she was doing something sweet for me, not realizing I was going to take it someplace dark, and not knowing how to handle it once I did.
While misguided, at least her lie was well-intentioned. That can't be said of my sixth-grade teacher who—on a field trip to Boston a couple of years later—told me that I "just missed Mary Tyler Moore" walking through Quincy Market while I was in the bathroom, and everyone got to say hi to her but me.

After I started weeping and threw my souvenirs in the garbage, however, she told me it was a joke.

I knew this was a shitty, mean joke. But I didn't care. All I cared about was that it didn't happen. Because that would be the worst thing, right? If Mary Tyler Moore and I were in the same place at the same time and just missed each other? I couldn't get over that.

Several years later, when I was in my mid-20s and living in Manhattan, my mom and cousins came in to visit from Queens and Long Island for a theater date on a July afternoon. As we exited our matinee, the usual Times Square sidewalk chaos was doubled by the fact that there were trucks lined up along the curb with cats and dogs up for adoption.

My mom's cousin looked at me with fear in her eyes: "I have to get out of here," she said. "If I don't leave now, I will adopt another dog and my husband will divorce me."

I understood this as my cue to get the suburbanites to less-intense territory, so I ushered everyone into a taxi to head back uptown for dinner and drinks, safe from whatever that scene was outside the theater.

But later that night when everyone left, I decided to do a "quick check" of Facebook before going to sleep, and I came upon some photos an acquaintance posted. I saw they were of those same dog and cat trucks, and that same crowd of people I was in, at the same time of day I was there. How amusing.

I started clicking around. But my amusement transformed to horror when three photos in, I saw her: Mary. Tyler. Moore. Standing in the same crowd I was in, unbeknownst to me. The worst thing that could never happen, happened.

In a fit of rage, I switched from Facebook to Google, turned on caps lock, and banged on my keyboard for answers: "MARY TYLER MOORE, SHUBERT ALLEY, JULY, WHY????!"

It took about two seconds to learn that the pet adoption situation we ran from earlier was Broadway Barks, an annual event hosted by Mary Tyler Moore and Bernadette Peters. Something I never heard of before, despite being the "biggest Mary fan in the world."

Like any normal person, I went to sleep feeling bereft and decided nothing mattered anymore and it would be fine to die.

But I woke up with a fresh perspective: Now that I knew about this event, I would just go next year! This is perfect. I found my way into Mary's life!

The following year, I showed up for Broadway Barks hours early. I secured a great spot in Shubert Alley. It was a typical hot, humid, rainy July morning in New York City. And soon the alley got crowded with wet people and wet dogs. Everything smelled. But I didn't care. I was doing this for Mary.

A few hours passed. The alley filled up. And it was time for Mary and Bernadette to come out and kick things off. My heart was in my throat and tears were resting in the corners of my eyes. I had a permanent smile fixed on my face. Here we go…

Out came the lovely Bernadette Peters:

"Welcome everybody!" she cooed.

"Thank you so much for coming!

"Unfortunately…

"Mary Tyler Moore cannot be here today…

"But we have Harvey Fierstein instead!"

A chorus of "awwww/aaahhh" fell over the crowd. But I was silent. With no offense to Harvey, my first reaction was just to smile bigger, thinking if I treated this as a joke it would become one.

But out came Harvey—and I knew it was over.

I squeezed my eyes shut the way I do when I need to go inside myself, expecting to feel devastated and to cry in front of all the wet people and dogs.

But instead, I felt something weird. I felt, fine? I even felt a little relieved.

I was fixated on meeting Mary for so many years, but it wasn't until this moment that I thought about what it would even mean to meet her now. It hit me that whatever I would get from it couldn't compare with what she gave me years ago when she appeared on my TV and helped me feel connected to something when I needed it most.

While we never met in this life, Mary Tyler Moore is still a part of me. And I am forever grateful to her for helping me feel less alone as a kid, and for making me think that I might just make it after all.

PAULINE FINDLAY

Momma Don't Think I See

Momma sits behind the weeping willow tree
          weeping
                    she think I can't see her weeping
that seeps
to the root of the tree.

I don't grasp the sobbing and hurt
          red bloated eyes that feels damp on
the rim of her sleeved coat.

Dead end dreams that lay in her head,
          and a father that didn't wed
her
             since he's found another's bed

Money's short
Bills go unpaid
          Never ask for handouts
              but works for pimp ass
Johnny down the lane

Momma scrubs toilets in the day
lifts her skirt at night
          prays to God on Sunday
              acting like life's gonna be
alright

But momma sits behind the weeping willow tree
          weeping
                    she think I can't see her weeping
that seeps
to the root of the tree

I would love to put my hand on her shoulder, and say
                  "Momma this rough time will soon be over, but just in
case
I have this green clover. God will shower us with His blessings
                and will pour down when He opens the heavens."

I'm sure she won't hear the reassurance of my voice

cause it'll get lost in the stillness of her saddened thoughts

Momma tries her best but life's got her beat,

and she can't see the hope beyond that damned willow tree.

Life's full of wonder if we could just hold on a little while longer.
But what can you say to a momma who sits by a weeping willow tree,
          weeping
                  if she doesn't have anything left
she believes in...

HOWARD FINGER

When the Last Glacier Melts

When the anti-science hacks get their way,
when our Congress defunds the EPA,
when we opt out of the climate change pact,
will this merely be the opening act?

Who among us then shall be taking stock,
cognizant of the ticking of the clock?
Will someone be watching over the flock?
What's going to become of the third rock?

When loud cries of outrage are not voiced then,
will the opportunity come again?
or will it be too late as time passes?
Will the do-gooders get off their assess?

When climate change finally takes its toll,
will the deniers still expose clean coal?
Will they urge us to dig a deeper hole?
Will we be wise to their sinister goal?

When there are no more polar bears, good God,
'cept for the Inuit, who'll find it odd?
Will the "nouveau riche" lament at Cape Cod,
and pause in pursuit of the perfect bod?

When the Great Barrier Reef's turning white,
and there are fewer sharks left that will bite,
will the masses finally see the light?
Will it lead more of them to join the fight?

When sea-level rises and the high tide
buries everything along the seaside,

even Mar-a-Lago, where will they hide?
Will all the nay-sayers take it in stride?

When lakes and rivers begin to die out,
due to the acid rain and prolonged drought,
will there be any shadow of a doubt
when the question's asked, why there are no trout?

When there are more tornadoes, hurricanes,
blizzards, tsunamis and torrential rains,
will the hypocrites believe what they see,
or will they shut their eyes and let it be?

When mosquito borne illnesses mushroom,
and unthinkable epidemics loom,
will the know nothings, once again, pooh-pooh
the dangers, insisting it's all untrue?

When the conspiracists run out of lies,
excuses, distortions and alibies
to cover up our planet's demise,
will anyone be taken by surprise?

When the last glacier melts, what can be said?
Afterwards, will mankind be seeing red?
Will the green movement finally be dead?
What will do-gooders latch onto instead?

CHRISTINA FITZPATRICK

Boston Rooftop

Couples in cotton gab. About important parties, a person named Pete, and the particular breed of car they admire. A dog with a mop of ivory moves and stops.

Hands clasped; my friend stands beside the man who brought us here. He is small-faced, pear-shaped, wearing something similar to boating clothes. He has a soft-bristled demeanor, fortified by the white shag rug in his living room and a gleaming watch that has gold dashes instead of numbers. My friend talks to his friends as if she will be a member of their troupe, drive in the backseat of their velvet cars, sit in their shaggy living rooms sipping cold, uninhibited wine.

In the sky: A mayflower, a blizzard of bees. No one says: *Oooh.* or *Ahhh.* Beer bottles sit wet in their hands.

A woman's ring makes a continuous clink against her Corona. She turns. What do you do? She asks.

I'm a writer.

A rider? She asks. *What* do you ride?

A writer, I say.

What do you write?

Books.

For children? She asks.

No.

A man appears beside us in loafers and pleated safari-shaded shorts. He sips his beer, without tilting his head. The Corona woman drifts away. I will see her later in the marble stairwell and her voice will call out to me like a slap: *Good luck.*

But now I am with a man wearing shorts fit for hunting tiger. His hair is receding and dry, parted like wind-blown grass. His arms thin, the blue bloodlines visible. I can see him as a child, his elbows on the table, an empty plate before him. He asks me the same question: What do you do? And the ivory dog appears beside him, sniffing the deck tiles.

The man touches its head carefully and the dog's dark mouth opens.

EMBER FLAME

The Drop

I'm sitting on a little ledge swinging my legs
swinging my legs off the edge
the drop beckons like a lover calling
hello my darling
you big brawny
you clear morning
you voluptuous excess
it tells me what I am
it is a place where I can die
dig about and feel my depth
yes, there is an inkling
a dim star in my belly
but fear is a force field between me
and the black
black, glittering abyss
I stroke all my things
machine made stuff with sharp edges gathering dust
I'm running out of space up here
yet I'm still so greedy to fill it up
I yearn to unsquish
to be loose and limbless
but I'm stuck sweating over false choices
dripping divine sweat onto the small stuff
my legs swing bravely
but my good cop bad cop
are backs against the wall
sensing their annihilation
in the bigness beneath
it's a terrible temptation to think I can be
as boundless as love
that I'm both brittle and brawn
brawn and brittle

I clench my hands
and say I'm not ready to be the gnarled tree
and savannah plain
to read the hieroglyphics of my heart in clay-mottled cliffs
but I'm still swinging my legs off this edge
and I have pins and needles as I inch closer
to that sweet, perfect bottomless pit

KOFI FOSU FORSON

Sitting with Keith at a Bar on A

Some guys walk easy, they don't strut, they are one with the ground
They are a walking flag pole, tattooed and torn, blowing in the wind
Eye of a pirate, pissed on street corners, waited on broken bombshells
Sometimes straddling a rhythm guitar, dirty jeans, wicked alligator smile
Leather skin, British boy good looks, Marlborough lip, tobacco tongue
Come dirty like a knife, shaking the reggae off the street, Rasta boys
No bodyguards, no lifeguards, looking death in the eye, laughing
The tall and thins, slip in like fins of sharks, gritting bloody teeth
On the dark corners they fight with breaths so hard, move to the beat

In walks Keith, rock and roll ghost, perpetual smoke pours from his lip
Puts his arm out for the usual, bartender nods in agreement, the regulars
Make like regulars, playing cool by the jukebox, playing pool in the light
All at attention, he's angling over, locking up a doo-wop tune, so soon
He calls up a girl to dance, body tight, match light, groping the way down
Falling for him, stranger, dolled up just enough, in her eyes, a magic puff
Backing away, he stands there watching her dance alone, smoke lifting
Original Van Gogh, painting her with his eyes, ashes builds at the tip
No Jumping Jack Flash, no Rolling Stones, cockeyed and wonderful
Blues on a Monday night, thump thumping through a seduced bar crowd
Here to see Billy go at it again, his band is really big shit, yeah, yeah
To my left is a Marley man, to my right is Keith, tap tapping his knee skin
Jiggling the cubes in a glass, smoking a rocket ship cigarette, blazing
His face is a weather map, takes me through Tahiti to the cold under
Whispers something in my ear, can't understand, bob bobbing my head
Smoking a rocket ship cigarette, alarming, he blows a whistle into the air
Loud and above it, I give Billy the fist pump, look at me, I got Keith
Sitting beside me, orange and blue, like a decked hammy boy bitchin'

So, like he doesn't stay for the encore, makes his way out before Billy
There on stage smashing his guitar, Keith would have liked that, maybe
He wasn't Live at Leeds, he was cool with a cigarette, held that baby
down

Played the chords so easy, always hammering down, lighting up a crowd
Never saw him play live, here on A he never bothered to strap it up
Just walked in on us when we least expected, sat, listened on, dangerously
We were the lucky ones, never saw Mick, Charlie or Ronnie, we saw
Keith
Sitting there with a smoke, glass of firewater and cubes, playing himself
A delicate British gentleman, walking wounded, crazy with the days

JASON GALLAGHER

Or At Least

You said you would help and heal me
from now until forever or
at least until tomorrow.

You told me to take each of my tomorrow's one day at a time or
at least to try.
You told me that the future wasn't important
to wade into the water only up to your today or
at least only dip my feet into your tomorrow.

And I noticed you needed healing too.
The forest of your eyes, brown, not green, seemed to confirm the need for
my reassuring silence,
            or
at least my ability to support the strength that courses behind those eyes.
As recently as this morning, I thought all my love lyrics had gone dry.
That I had fallen into matrimony to find the feelings too unfathomable or
at least found the comfort no artistic match for the thrill.

However, there is no need for another Dionysian monument to sweaty
palms
when your kisses give me the final answer or
at least the possibility of redemption.

The contradictions have made me realize that I didn't know anything
about what I've liked or
at least what I liked before today.
We watch TV that I wouldn't have been allowed to watch and
we marvel at how different it would have been or
at least it would have seemed if we'd gotten together earlier.

I will sit with you now everyday while you watch your dog videos

Although I've no interest in dog videos, or the 21st century, or
at least up to this point.

ART GATTI

Crash

Knock them young bones
'gainst the old
Boychild jumping
on Grandpa's lap

Crunching thigh bones…
Riding like the wind

I know you rider gonna miss me when I'm gone

No sense of life, no thought of endings
Just being
Just night, followed by day and the inevitable
next night

I know you rider gonna miss me when I'm gone

A face
A presence
A stubbly beard
Feel a feeling of Grandpa

I know you rider gonna miss me when I'm gone

JENNIFER HARMON GERSBECK

Light & Dark

It's deep down inside me from long ago.
Not channeled at him, my dad, little Jenny-me OR God,
Yes, of course it's channeled at them at US!

Rage Blooms within ME!
Rage
Blooms
within
ME

I buried the anger in the desert
and covered it with beautiful magenta flowered cactus
I cut my finger on the sharp needles
of self - doubt
Labeling myself average, unorganized, chubby.

Fuck that, I am mesmerizing!

Growing up
I was
Angry about
His infidelity
Her blindness
What I could not control

"RAGE BLOOMS WITHIN ME!"

My eyes have it. Camouflage, golden green swirl, metallic.
My eyes are a bath tub to wash in, a swimming pool of acrylic war paint
Roll over
I am covered in tattoos only I can see.
No Secrets,

I soak in faith to relax sore muscles,
Leave with a natural shine

TAKE ALL OF ME.
Triumph is built on
going there to

"Rage Blooms Within ME!"

I am proud to make this grand announcement.

The day arrived when I rescued myself.

I am capable
I am free.

Dear Dad,

Thank you for loving me.
Thank you for showing me love.

Thank you for letting me be real and true.
Thank you for encouraging me.

Thank you for not holding my frustration or anger against me.
Thank you for letting me be authentic.
Thank you for letting me do exactly what I needed to do.

VOGUE GIAMBRI

sometimes I think of eating jazz on Monday mornings

I'm *undecided,* tell me have you thought
anything about the *anatomy of a*
murder   my *mood*
is repulsive and what a hangover
I've reeled today and yesterday you
took my *body and*
soul is something I've been
thinking about   you
have been away (not so far!)
I came over in my pajamas
peeling clementines you hate
the smell and how funny! I am dripping
juice all over the couch you
never sit on because Boaz
fucked here   once
we cuddled when no one was home
we're only *alone together* don't
make me cry I remember
all your gigs and won't you
kiss me once *while we're*
young and delusional I
promise *there will never be*
another you   broke
my typewriter trying to fix
my heart hurts thinking
its so cold and you live so far
away my bikes locked
downstairs I have no key
don't yell at me you're always *ramblin'*
about *lonely women* it's not funny
eventually I'll leave *just*
for you I'd stop singing *honey*

suckle rose and you won't hurt
me like bruised knees making
giant steps its fine we will just be
in love with each other
secretly my favorite things
are those you hate
playing the sax for me
like sonny always screaming in my
ear I saw the way you looked
free and Connor's coming over
today she told me how
you feel silly without
me – *raincheck?*
and we're out of *bird food*
but that doesn't mean you
can take my cereal and you're so
loud with your *bird calls*
that mean nothing and   everything
sounds like it means
I have no *money in my pocket*
and you have no way home
the *alternate take* of
you *love*
your spell
is everywhere

ROBERT GIBBONS

No Artist Statement

I disappear among the tourist
washed ashore like a lobster pot
see the stain of a tanning salon
the sunburn ocean, the kayak
and the beach towel, the monitor
by a traffic cop in Shropshire, it wanders
in strips and pretends in stanzas

this art becomes a workshop, so be
careful in the detail, the anchor
or the sail, rather muse in winter
then the center will find me
here is the one at the art gallery
that hold the galley, the ones
with nine collection of verse or
versus

they are educated and rehearsed
claim not judgment, but decline
the emotion of conflict or interest
is still pensive, but

I am within reach, a stray doubloon
found on a beach as skeletal
as a sea shell could be a raze
a dune shack without water, there
is still disorder

yet, there is no artist statement required
rather a commune with the wharf, the drift
wood from Vermont, form anew
in this overworked ground
there can still be a marriage

between glass and wood, it is
more about the light than the
technical, but all is accidental

Alas, save me in this workshop
this found poem has presence
reborn, all over again, the
revelation still speaks to me,
the image will never tell me
where to go.

GORDON GILBERT JR.

This is NOT How It's Going to End!

That's what I'm thinking as I make the call to 911. I'm sitting on the stoop at 15 Cornelia St. For a few minutes, I've been in denial.

Phillip's *What the Hell Is Love?* program ended downstairs at the cafe at 7:30 pm.

Earlier, I had done my five minutes at the mic, and was rewarded with warm applause. I was feeling perfectly fine, except that I'd finished my glass of wine an hour ago, and I was thirsty.

So when I'm making my exit, talking to a few friends as I pass by, my first thought, when I feel the constriction in my throat, is that it's heartburn, and I ask the man behind the bar for a glass of water. It's cold, and feels good as I drink it down, but I only feel worse after.

I make my way to the stairs, passing some other friends. I tell them I don't feel good and I'm going home to lie down. As I climb the stairs, the most incredible pain begins under both arms down to my fingers.

Upstairs, I rudely push past a waiter, making my way through the crowd and out onto the street. The pain under my arms is now excruciating, unlike anything I've ever felt before. As I approach 15 Cornelia, only forty yards down from the café, I have to sit down. I realize that even if I make it home, lying down until I feel better is no longer an option.

I remember reading somewhere not every heart attack involves chest pain; sometimes it's pain in one of the arms. And I'm having pain in *BOTH*! So, I make the call to 911, thinking, this is *NOT* how it's going to end!

Time stretches, seconds dragging out as the phone rings, and then I'm telling the man I think I'm having a heart attack, and I'm answering his questions. He tells me help is on the way. We end the call.

After an eternity, but maybe only a few minutes, I see flashing lights at the other end of Cornelia, but *NOT* coming down the street! I can't believe it! Someone got the address wrong?! I force myself up off the stoop and walk toward the flashing lights. But now I see three firemen coming my way, one carrying an oxygen tank. I stop and wait, and we walk together back to the stoop. I realize their fire truck could not make the turn.

They give me oxygen, check my pulse, blood pressure. Suddenly the ambulance is here. A young woman and slightly older man get out and take over. The firemen help EMS put me on a stretcher and roll me into the ambulance. I thank them as they leave. Inside, the EMS continue the oxygen and take an EKG reading, and we are on our way to Beth Israel, him driving, her monitoring my signs.

I'm wheeled right through emergency into an elevator, up to a higher floor, and into what must be an operating room, where two doctors and some others are waiting. The pain abates as a local anesthetic kicks in. I'm awake throughout the entire procedure, a detached observer, as they run a catheter up through a wrist artery, look around, and decide upon a course of action.

Minutes later, it's over, and I'm in a recovery room, a stent in the artery that had been blocked by plaque. Blood is flowing to that part of the heart again, and I'm experiencing an overwhelming sense of relief: the pain is gone. They never removed my wristwatch. I look at the time. It's 8:30 pm. Less than an hour from when I felt the first symptoms.

They will tell me that the damage to the heart muscle was minimal, because so little time had elapsed before they started the flow of blood again. The ordeal is over, and I'm now on the long road to a full recovery.

That feeling of personal immortality many of us have, who have never been seriously ill? Well, that delusion is gone forever!

So, this is *NOT* how it ends. I've been given a second chance.

God bless the firemen first responders, the EMS, the cardiologist who put in the stent, all the wonderful staff at Beth Israel.

If tonight was to be my last performance, and that it was done here at the Cornelia Street Café, I could be satisfied with that, but now I know it's not, and there is still so much I want to do.

Lying here in the recovery room, I'm already thinking if anyone asks me, I'll tell them

that if you are going to have a heart attack, I can't think of a better place than at the Cornelia Street Café. Hell, you're only minutes away from Beth Israel.

Just remember to go outside before you call 911. You know how Robin is about using your cellphone in the café!

Oh, and I'm on 7 meds now, one of which has the potential side effect of forgetfulness.

Best excuse ever!

JOEL LOUIS GOLD

Janet

The wind of doubt visits her small chamber as she dresses for the night. Why I made this date is beyond me? Am I still the orphaned child without substance, a transparent girl still needing adult permission before I tell the truth before I act on what I want before the anxiety builds and sticks it to me making me feel like the little girl, I haven't been for forty years. Amazing I have done as well as I have as well as I have let myself become, amazing.

Janet Greene brushes her thick brown mane. Privileged follicles of DNA catch the delicate tungsten light creating a momentary halo a crown of deception that seduces the eye while tricking the mind pulling thought into a cul-de-sac of pleasure than moving on leaving the witness empty and alone wanting to see what is no longer there addicted to the mysterious sensuality building a conundrum a moat of time to be crossed at a later date. Janet's hair, a Mobius strip with no beginning, no end the envy of the women who depend on her. All the successful frightened women who call her at odd times of the night wanting Janet to plug them back into their source of power belief their generators of life.

Janet, a Harvard graduate in the physics department, was a devout believer in the cosmos of second chances reflected in a changing universe, an atomic clock moving slowly but inevitably in an unattainable void-creating new worlds, birthing cyclones of inestimable wonder filling one's imagination with a mathematical reverence for balance and as yet unnamed chaotic explosions resulting from the madness of unlimited space and a calm inevitability a parturition of belief that soothes the fears of the unknown. From the biting world of science, Ms. J. A. Stein took a master's degree in psychology moving from outer space to inner space a world as complicated and universal as a lost planet beyond the incomparable surveillance of the Hubble telescope. Her practice bloomed with the urgency and beauty of a rose. Word of mouth, from one mended damaged soul to another wounded human needing a path of release from a labyrinth of pain and confusion, spread quickly until her name was scrawled across a wall of graffiti in block red letters on the upper West

Side of NYC. WHEN IN DOUBT SHOUT HER OUT AJ
STEIN.........! What shall I wear to this date who should I be on this
Stonehenge moment in my stalled life? Janet called Magic by those who
know her those who have experienced the intellectual prestidigitator the
alchemist of reality transforming dark catastrophe into a mushroom cloud
of light moves slowly through her rococo living room. Floor to ceiling
windows surround the lighted box lined with the art that speaks to her
soothes her doubts and creates a terrain of calm. Expensive prints of
Matisse, Modigliani, Rothko, Pollack & de Kooning a cultural topography
that seduces her senses. Behind her India Ink eyes a Vesuvius of pent up
images build silently waiting for its opening planning for the day when all
will break away and hold her in its treacherous pincers atop a Freudian
wall about to crumble an inevitable fall into a psychic bog a quick sand of
hibernating thoughts best placed in her ever available darkness of fear and
warped sensibilities. The tsunami of truths she meticulously masks with
success and deep self-satisfaction will one day burst when she least
expects it but always knew it would emerge to define her time on this
Earth leaving her with her last moment of consciousness her last breath of
history all alone in a cradle of sadness and regret in an eternal womb of
memory.

MY G-D what the Hell am I thinking? What price must I pay for a just
little bit of pleasure? Don't I deserve an anonymous thimble of
contentment a modicum of grace an atom sized push of sensuality a
quieting of the heart an easy lovely bloom of satisfaction and an
unperturbed mini rush of self- love. There, I have thought it and now I am
going to say it out loud. I deserve to be happy. The opera of her fantasies
hits the high C of acceptance transforming this room of highly controlled
human consequence into a rout of improvisational joy. A Tarpeian hop
skip and jump accompanied by a fortissimo of musical chairs with one
eternal empty chair waiting for her without debate or punishment a reward
for just being alive. She takes one long last look in the full- length mirror
that is sometimes her enemy sometimes her bride. She is pleased turns off
the lights and moves silently through the dark crossing the Rubicon of
doubt knowing she will never go back.

RUSS GREEN

Fatherland

Solace on the other side
of the sound. Waiting for the bottom
to come up, for the fish to drag
the interminable whale of childhood

scars to the surface. The beating
of wild drums echoes through the rib cage.
Escape from the lock-step, jackboot heel
crushed gardenias in the flowerbed

that was my flesh. Jackboot heel crushed
candy canes that were my bones. Jackboot
heal crushed my crayons I used to brighten my lonely

canvass. That jackboot heel sent a blitzkrieg
through the sky, pierced the sun with bolts
of lightning, burned my joy. You

burned my joy. I want it back. You spilled
my blood, stretched me 'til I cracked.
Splattered eyeballs across a once free shining

dance floor. Jackboot clinging to the night.
This dark molasses memoir, a film noir. A sea
of names I could have cut a rug with now languishes

among the broken barnacles and dried blood
of washed up mollusks, crashing
possibilities against the sure-footed
captain's feet. I hop over gunnels, climb

to the safety of the wheelhouse. The helmsman's

yelling at me to grab the wheel while he battens the hatches.
He screams, "Ya gotta take those waves head on
man or it's all over!"

Surfing the crests, pounding between waves
until the parting of heavenly chaos. Peaceful waters.
The jackboot heels.

Floating. Broken. Sinking. Gone.

CHRISTOPHER GRIGSBY

The Avenue

To think that it could come to this.
To cross one more right off your list
To cross one bridge into the night
where right is wrong
and wrong is right

To think that what is good is true
To walk that dreaming avenue
To think and feel and disregard
what hurts too much
and hits too hard

To jump and shout upon the thought
that what we want is what we ought
that felt alone, there still is love
and those who've gone
are still above

To cast the past into the now
To crave the one that won't allow
To wonder who and why and how
and think it all was done by chance
for heavy sighs and failed romance

To give a gift unto thine hand
To prostrate proud at thy command
To rise like phoenix when we stand
for commonwealth upon this land
- that we might build what we demand

That we may eat until we fill
That we shall leave and pay no bill
That we should dream of all this
and still know pain
where we crave bliss

To make a list and check it twice
To feed the flame and pay the price
To think we see what's good and true
of pharaoh and of ingénue

Whose outlines you and I once knew
as we dance into the blue
along the dreaming avenue

BRENDALIZ GUERRERO

Death in the Time of Flowers

Know this

All the blossoms that spring forth from me

Will have you running through their veins

You, my giving ground

My fertile soil

Who wrought me?

As many blooms before

And offered your few raindrops

In exchange for rainstorms with holy church thunderclaps

To shake my roots

Awaken my spirit to reach the sun

And commune with the Goddess in me

So that I may laugh & kiss life onto others

But at what cost?

To see & feel your growth

At the behest of your withering?

Of your groans, creaks & moans?

In an act of defiance

I wish to retract my leaves

Bury myself back in

Beg the sky to make fertilizer of this stem

So that you may rise

And crown me compost

So that you may smile upon me once more

This joyous cycle ends in nothing

But sorrow

For as much as I beg to keep you here

There's only so much water I can offer before we BOTH run dry

I love you.... you may go...

Just promise me ONE thing

Promise that you'll leave a petal at my doorstep

You all the same

JOHN S. HALL

Invisible Dog

My dog is invisible, but he follows me around wherever I go. He takes invisible pisses on the lawn next door and my neighbor never knows. He takes a shit in the middle of the sidewalk and nobody sees and nobody cares and nobody notices when they step in it. He barks and only I can hear it. He does incredible tricks that only I can enjoy. He eats invisible food that I buy at the invisible supermarket with my invisible money that I make at my invisible job, where I sit at an invisible desk doing nothing all day. When I come home, my dog wags his invisible tail and showers me with invisible kisses, and I love the odorless smell of his invisible dog breath. My invisible dog is very, very, old, but when he dies, it will be basically the same as it is now, as if he were still here with me.

L.R. LAVERDE HANSEN

The Magical Man

Sandila looked increasingly despondent with each sip. Her eyes kept darting back and forth between her wine and the screen on her smartphone. He said it was over, but Brady had said that before. He would sometimes threaten, sometimes take off for a few days, but he would always return. Now it had been a week, and Brady hadn't responded.

Sandila didn't want to believe that. Sure, he had his issues, but Brady was her man. Tall, athletically built, Ivy-League educated and a corporate lawyer, he was everything a socially ambitious yet politically moderate girl could want. He wasn't rude to her friends. He impressed her parents. He was even good at foreplay. Brady was all for staying in New York City until she was settled in her career, so they could have that baby and shop for that family house in Connecticut. He was as perfect as any Jewish man with a WASPY name could possibly be.

Then Lizette came into the picture. Lizette Negrón, that fucking Puerto Rican or Dominican bitch from Mount Vernon! She was his legal secretary, for Christ's sakes! Sandila knew that something might be up, but she couldn't be sure.

Then she saw the Facebook picture. It was Brady and Lizette at some *Sociedad Latina* party somewhere in Manhattan. They were both covered in sweat from salsa dancing. The thing that got her wasn't the nature of their pose or embrace. It was how ecstatic Brady looked in the picture. He looked a kind of happy he never did before.

Now Brady wasn't answering. He must be busy. He couldn't just leave Sandila like this. This was the weekend she had been planning for weeks. He must be having second thoughts or was under some stress. You never throw away a good thing for a fling. Brady was so much more than that.

But Sandila wasn't getting any answer. Her calls weren't blocked, so that was good, but why no response? She didn't get it. She had planned a beautiful getaway to Longwood Gardens outside of Philly. Brady claimed he was into horticulture and botany and all that shit, so why wasn't he more excited by this trip? She just didn't get anything anymore.

Again, he wasn't responding. Sandila pushed the sadness away by again reaching for the glass. She was up to her fourth. The bartender, who had been chatting with some regulars, couldn't help but notice. Experience told him this wasn't going to end well, but he was game to please the young lady. Maybe he felt sorry for her. Maybe he was glad that she was ordering Riesling instead of Chardonnay. Either way, he had the next bottle ready to open when she gave the word. Then he might close her tab with a final toast.

The wine wasn't working for Sandila. Nothing was working for her now. She had called her girlfriend Mindy, but Mindy was spending her weekend with *her* boyfriend in Pennsylvania. Brady had killed their double date, and the damn tickets were nonrefundable. So here was Sandila, stuck, not wanting this situation from hell. Though it was useless, she gulped another swig. The bartender's fingers practically caressed the bottle's cork. Then a guy squeezed past Sandila in order to order three beers. The bartender ditched the bottle and started pouring the pints. This guy was clearly smaller than Brady and more casually dressed, though he was no hipster. He did offer his excuses to Sandila, but that wasn't what caught her eye. He smiled a broad, bright irony-free smile that she hadn't seen from a young man in years.

Sandila scanned the bar area. She saw that he was sitting at a table—alone. She couldn't help herself.

"So you're going to have all those beers by yourself?"

"Well, the bartender said there's a minimum credit card payment, so I figure why not catch up with my drinking."

Sandila thought of making a crack about him being an alcoholic but after four wines, she might not have a barstool leg to stand on. So she zipped it and smiled back.

The guy smiled again and took his drinks back to his seat. Sandila couldn't help noticing him. He wrote on his laptop, but with a joyous and feverish passion she thought at first was a put on. But that wasn't all. After a while, he tapped the table and clapped his hands like a madman. He just looked like a child who had found the essential secret to life. And every now and then, when not typing, when not smiling or swaying or drinking, he looked up and aimed his eyes straight at her. Sandila was taken aback by the glowing intensity in the man's gold and green eyes. She realized as offbeat as he was, he looked handsome by the light of his laptop.

Normally she would have waited. She would have made the man come to her. But after everything that had happened: a scumbag boyfriend; a weekend gone to pot; a growing loss of control to the wine, she was now insanely curious. What the hell was that boy writing about anyway? And why was he smiling so much at her?

She couldn't wait any more. She would either find out or keep looking at a phone that was not going to look back. Sandila closed her tab, tipped the bartender, and boldly strode to his table. She sat down right across from him, her bright brown eyes hooking up with his.
For a moment she paused. Then Sandila turned her head to the side, all curious.

"So what are you writing about on that laptop?"

The young man smiled yet again. "Well, it's a short story. It's about this girl. She's at a bar, checking her phone in frustration, waiting for her life to change."

HOLLY HEPP-GALVAN

Stones

All old ladies have good stories, but mine is better than most. You see, I was Little Red Riding Hood. Yes. People all over the world have heard how I set off in the woods in a red cloak bearing a basket of goodies for my grandmother. It's strange, though. No one ever asks what *became* of Little Red Riding Hood. No one asks what happened after she emerged from the hot, sticky furnace of the wolf's belly and was forced to watch as the huntsman filled him with stones. It was a gruesome thing, really. The huntsman kept carrying them in, armful after armful, from Granny's garden. He made me hold the wolf's front paws while Granny held the back. And even after the wolf was full of stones, still he brought in more, laughing as he shoved them around the wolf's heart and on to his liver. Smiling as he squeezed sharp pebbles by his spleen. Why? Why answer cruelty with cruelty? You have saved two lives, why weigh down another's?

But even as it grew dark, the huntsman persisted. He was a brutal man with one eye that had been picked clean by a woodpecker. And when he couldn't see outside, he started putting in pieces of my Granny's pottery – small bowls and china cups with pictures of cherries, milk-glass swans, and ceramic dancers with their arms upraised. Piece by piece he wedged them into the wolf's wet insides – tiny squirrel figurines, and cherubs with harps.

The wolf was silent the whole time. He stayed completely still and watched me with his big black eyes. Only once did I hear him murmur, and when I bent down to those great, white teeth I heard him say just one word, "Mercy."
Eventually, the huntsman was done. He went over to Granny's sewing box and took a needle and thread to sew up the wolf's belly. He made big, ugly stitches that strained against the swollen pink skin. And then somehow the wolf managed to drag himself out of the cottage and down to the river.

But what people don't know is that the wolf didn't drown that day. Nor the next. He just lay there in the cold water with his paw holding onto a rock. He lay there with his swollen belly and his wet fur. He lay there motionless and gazed at the sky. I went to visit him most days. I don't know why. There was something about his stillness, his heaviness. We just sat together and listened to the water gurgling and watched the trees swaying in the breeze.

Then one day, the wolf said, "I'm hungry." And it didn't strike me as strange because wolves are always hungry. It's their nature. But I didn't know what to feed him because I didn't want to kill another animal. So I reached into the river and pulled out a smooth stone. And without a word, the wolf opened his mouth and swallowed it.

After that, I started feeding him a new stone each day. It became my mission, my passion, to find the best stones. I searched everywhere. I brought him shiny stones with bits of silver. I brought him small speckled stones like bird's eggs. I brought him smooth stones and pitted stones and stones with rings. I brought him stones with stripes of color and ones that were jet-black. I searched all over the countryside and through the woods. As I got older, I took trains to new towns and found stones that had tumbled down from mountains. In other countries, I found stones that had traveled in glaciers or been hacked out of a mine. I found stones that had been in boy's pockets and stones that had been thrown during protests. And one day, when I was about the age Granny had been, I went to the river to find the wolf so weighed down with stones that only the tip of his nose and his eyes were still above the water. He was monstrously huge at this point, like a fallen tree, like a grey boulder - he filled the river from bank to bank and only his tail still swished in the current.

At that moment, I realized that the story needed to end. That we both needed to let go. So, I took a pair of scissors and carefully cut the old stitches on the wolf's belly. And as soon as I did, his skin sprang back and the stones heaved upward. There was a mountain of stones. And I waded into the river and started taking them out. One by one I reached in and collected them. The shiny ones, and the grey ones, and the ones with holes. I piled them around me. The round ones and the smooth ones, and the ones like little embryos with their eyes just forming. It took me over a year, but finally, I got close to his heart. And then I started pulling out the original stones from Granny's garden and the china cups and the little squirrel figurines. I carefully pulled them all out and placed them beside me.

And when I pulled out the last one, the wolf heaved a huge sigh. His body now floated lightly on the top of the water. His great belly was empty. And without a word, he let go of the bank with his paw. He let go, and instantly the current swept him downstream. He floated lightly and easily, his body turning in circles and rocking from side to side. He floated like a leaf, like a feather, like a torn page from a book. He floated down the river and out of sight. And as I watched him go, I thought that this, THIS is how the story should end.

JUDITH LEE HERBERT

Letter to My Father

When you lay wounded in the snow
in Bastogne, alone among the fir trees,
so cold and wet and numb,
wondering if someone would come,
or if you would die—
tell me how you held on.

You told me only about General McAuliffe.
how, when surrounded and asked to surrender,
he said, "Nuts!"
You savored his brazen word of defiance.

Mom has lost the plaque honoring
that battle, along with your Bronze Star Medal
and Purple Heart. She is confused and asks
where she lives, and when she is going home.
Dana leaves for college in the fall.
Allan has turned seventy-one.
And you are gone seventeen years.

I search inside myself
for that force in you, knowing
your blood runs through me.

ANN HERENDEEN

Gooseberries

The earliest lives I remember were in the eastern lands, wet and fertile with rice and fish; civilized worlds of manners and art and cleanliness. But there were too many of us for the land to support, and some of us had to move.

We traveled along the steppe, a desert of grass. We learned to ride horses and to herd goats and sheep, a few cattle. We drank their milk and, when they were old, slaughtered them and gorged on the meat. Those were festivals! My mouth always waters at the smell of roasting flesh.

I was a king's daughter. That is, my father called himself a king. But we were poor. A man had to stay put to be a king, to rule over the others too wretched to move, trapped on the dry land that can only grow grass. And people can't eat grass.

When my mother died, brittle and pale as winter hay, my father married again, and soon I had two sisters. The younger was harmless, mild and slow. But the older one was like me. It was as if she had a third eye: she missed nothing. When our mother sent us out to pasture with our one little red cow, only a crust of gritty bread to eat, my sister caught me bowing to the animal, drinking the milk from her udder. Once in a while I would cut a hole in her shoulder to suck the blood as it pulsed near the skin. Hot and sweet! I could feel its warmth inside me, nourishing my bones and my heart.

Perhaps I should have shared. But one little cow does not produce much milk, even less if she is bled, and if I was going to get out I needed to be strong, not good. That cow, her blood and milk, turned me from a starved girl into a fine woman, with high, round breasts and a belly that cried its red tears each month, mourning the child it had not been given.

So my sister told, and our little cow was slaughtered while she was still young, before her milk dried up. It was time for me to move on from this stupid family, my sisters thin and dirty, wrapping themselves in rags and hunched over with famine like peasants, their heads crawling with lice.

My father was kind, and he gave me some of the cow's guts, with the shit that would allow something else to grow on this sterile grassland. I grew berries. Sweet and juicy, like my body, that should not always be a barren steppe. The birds, who could move about as we used to, made nests in the bushes and guarded the fruit from all but me.

When Prince Ivan came to find a wife, only I could give him what he craved. He was the son of another self-styled king, but his family was richer than ours, living on the western edge of the steppe where more crops grew, and he had noblemen with vast holdings to pay him rent in kind.

I walked like a queen, straight-backed, head up, as I brought him the large bowl heaped with woman-fruit, womb-red and vein-purple, and I looked him full in the face. It was a good face: sharp and hard and no-nonsense about him. And wise. There's nothing to be gained from marrying a stupid man; any power he inherits he'll squander, the wife and children the first to be sacrificed. Prince Ivan didn't smile, but he lowered his eyelids in satisfaction at the wife who had chosen him.

We lived happily at first. My only source of disquiet was my husband's old tutor, Evgeny. Evgeny recognized me, my selfishness and my greed, although why that should bother me, I couldn't say. One night, when my husband did not come to my bed, I hunted him down and there he was, his mouth on that old man's cock, like a boy with his master. Ah, now I saw! When my husband was a youth, and Evgeny a man in his prime, that's how their love had been, nor had it ended all these years later.

When Ivan came to me the next night, I made sure he got me pregnant and I bore a son. *That* for Evgeny! But the tutor was a kind man, and my friend, and I should not have doubted him.

Everything was so good that I almost threw it away. I wanted to show my father all that had grown from his one act of compassion, and from our little red cow. I brought my son and my fine husband home for a visit—and that's when it happened. My false mother knew me, as Evgeny did, but without love, and she tempted me with a different kind of freedom, in order to put her daughter in my place.

Now I could move. Really move, as was in my blood, the blood of the nomads of the steppe. I flew with the geese, my shoulders growing the powerful muscles that allowed me to fly for a whole day without tiring, my wrists crooking into wings and my fingers elongating into pinions. Should I have guessed how hard it would be to shed that goose skin? I knew only that it was like emerging from a fetid mud hut on the first day of spring, soaring over those long green-gray fields, the winds bending the stalks in waves, like ripples on a big fishpond, when you throw a stone or a frog dives in--plop! As I flew away with my flock, honking and cackling with the joy of leaving that squalor behind, I had one dreadful thought: My son!

It took me the whole day to find my way back, and there he was, in Evgeny's shaking arms. I threw off my warm, waterproof, feathered skin and nursed him, both breasts. *Please, my beautiful boy, drink it all, for how will I ever find you again?*

A second day the same thing: the need to fly pulling me up and the love for my son dragging me back. This time my husband was waiting. "What did you think? That it's all the same to me, you or your sister?"

I was shivering, naked without my feathers. The smell of roasting flesh had me drooling, but it was my goose skin he was burning, to trap me as a woman, his wife. He caught me in his arms and I struggled, becoming every loathsome animal I could think of: a lizard, a snake, a frog, insects, but he would not let me go.

"If you wish me to give up my old friend, I will not. Not for you, not for anyone. The boy can thrive with a wet nurse, but what will I do without love?"

The fight went out of me. The only person to love like that had been my mother, and I had grown up too poor for generosity. But for him, I would try. My breasts and belly flattened and I took on a man's shape. I was a spindle.

My husband laughed at the smooth wooden prick--a woman's tool--in his hand. He snapped me in half and threw the pieces away, the top over his shoulder, behind him, and the bottom underarm, in front.

My sister, seeing me gone, climbed the fence to come to him, and he shot her, a barbed arrow through the heart. Now when they tell this story they say he used a gun, but this happened long ago, and I know what I heard as I crawled over the flattened grass, my two halves inching their way toward each other and rejoining: the ruffled whirr of the fledged arrow's flight and the crack when it split the breastbone. Perhaps his people were Scythians or Parthians once, like mine.

Now I can no longer fly, am no longer a nomad. I stay in one place, and if we need to travel, I ride in a cart pulled by a gelding. But I have my son, and the love of my husband. My boy will grow up wise and strong and sensible, like his father. Evgeny is teaching him. In the spring, I will be giving my husband a daughter.

BLAIR HOPKINS

Wreckage

George was quite comfortably fucked up at his regular dive but something wasn't sitting right inside. All the other regulars were here, he had command of the record player... It was the same Friday night he'd had a million times over but something was missing and he knew exactly what it was. Susanne hit the road that morning and he ached missing her. He hated to acknowledge it.

30 years old and he'd watched all his peers pass him by. He'd been to five weddings this fall. Everyone had good jobs and good-looking kids and here he was, watching the take-out bags and beer cans pile up around the nightstand in his childhood bedroom. He'd moved home after college to look after his mother, once a vibrant powerhouse of a woman who, in the wake of his father's disappearance, had been reduced to a life of gallon vodka jugs, unfiltered cigarettes, and episodic hysteria. Tonight, she was on a tear so he stayed out. 30 years old with no direction. 30 years old and his hands already shook until he'd put back a few whiskeys.

One thing had changed recently, though. He had this chick hanging around. George had been alone a long time but his buddy died last April and left a whole lotta pretty woman in need of comfort so he took up with one of 'em; Nearly a year later they were still at it. Susanne had a lotta feelings to work out and he didn't mind one bit her doing so on his dick. It was a relationship seeded in despair but they had in fact come to love each other so none of that really mattered.

You'd think they'd be a funny looking pair. He was an easy 5" shorter and she had about 40 lbs. on him, but they spend most of their time sitting on barstools or laying in bed so the aesthetics didn't really make any difference either. Anyone who stumbled across them could tell they had a fine ol' time.

"You make me feel like... I don't know. Like a man I guess." He remembered a few nights before, taking a drag off a joint and staring up at her. She was topless, straddling him. "I feel like I could actually do something for myself, you know? Maybe when I come down to New Orleans I just won't leave. Just stay and play music and eat and fuck."

"I'll help you get set up." Susanne took back the joint and leaned forward to lay her breasts over his face; they continued their high, lazy play. "I know people down there. You'd be happy. I'm happy. You have no idea. Fuck New York anyway."

He wrapped his arms round her waist and flipped her onto her back, burying his face in her neck and her startled laughter. "You're right. I'll be there by Fat Tuesday."

Loosing himself from the memory George throws back a shot of whiskey and eyes a trembling hand. "Fuck. I've gotta fix that." They say it at the same time, a thousand miles apart. It's 2 am on a dark stretch of I-59 just below Hattiesburg and Susanne's hands are shaking too; the tires on her little jalopy are bald and the alignment is bad enough that it's fucking up the steering. Driving is a lot more effort than it was a month ago.

They'd argued the night before she left, before and after the fucking. They didn't argue often but when they did it was always about the same thing: he wasn't ready for their relationship to get more serious and she wasn't keen on being reminded. She'd left New York to get her head together after a string of misfortune and was way more invested in George than she wanted to be; he was the only thing bringing her back around. It wore heavy on her mind as she tore down the highway. In the bathroom, George digs a key into a tiny plastic bag and thinks about the unwitting lie he told her. "I'll see you in New Orleans," he'd said as she grabbed her suitcase, eyes glistening.

"I'll miss you 'til you get there," she'd offered.

"I know."

He ain't gonna see her in New Orleans. His will to fulfill promises keeps disappearing up his left nostril. Back at his beer now, George knows he'll never make it south. He wants to. He wants to make her happy. He wants a shot at his own happiness. But he won't make it. "She'll get over it. I'll see her soon enough. She'll forgive me."

With a sudden and sickening clunk, the front right tire ejects itself from the wheel well. Susanne is working the tired out of her eyes at the time and doesn't have time to gasp, let alone troubleshoot. The jalopy careens into the ditch at 80 mph and flips.

Dazed, she pulls herself from the wreckage and into the beam of the headlights, fumbling for her phone but she's dizzy and tired so sinks to her knees, eventually laying her head down in the wet grass, soothed by its coolness against the humidity of the Mississippi night. Blood mixing with the green under the golden headlight beam prompts loose a pained sigh. She's gonna let go, gonna just let herself dream about Mardi Gras.

Another hour and a few more whiskeys and Geroge'll be doing the same.

VICKI IORIO

I Didn't Say I Didn't Love Him

He promised me a lady's pearl handle 22
if I married him. Next time you're in Cleveland
look up Jimmy, the best man at my wedding,
living an Andy Hardy life with his wife in Shaker Heights

which I hear is da bomb
like Long Island's North Shore or the Hamptons
tony without Tony, my Italian husband

who thinks hydroponic tomatoes are the work of the devil-
only shit in the soil can grow the real thing. He makes
his own wine and plucks figs from the tree in our
Brooklyn backyard.

You think this is as idyllic
as being the wife of a sheep herder
who looks like Liam Neeson on some island dot
off the thumb nail of Scotland.

After ten years of marriage
he wants to do me doggie style on the living room floor
while he watches the Mets
(my therapist calls this the marital tipping point)

He calls it a double header matinee.
I'd like to slit his cock open with a glass shard from my chardonnay
but he belts me first and I cool my shiner with a frozen steak.

I am buying a bus ticket to Cleveland.
Jimmy's wife said she'll set me up in an apartment
with furniture from her basement
and a cuckoo clock that does not judge.

JERRY T. JOHNSON

A Poem for the Road

today i travel by plane across the country

whether by plane, whether by train
whether by ship i enjoy a sense of adventure

this morning i'm at O'Hare on my way to Detroit
and as i stand at my gate gazing at my surroundings
i spot an interesting and remarkable sight

there is a young man seated at a table
in a coffee shop facing the concourse
typing on a typewriter

he's typing away on a beautiful
blue as a cloudless morning sky
typewriter

of course, i must stop by and say "hello"

i tell him, "you know you are going to attract
a pack of tourists, banging away
on that thing like that"

smiling a broad smile, he says, "i certainly hope so"

then i tell him, "well write on you writing warrior, write on"

he tells me that he is writing letters while he awaits his flight
we talk about writing, poetry and prose
we shake hands as i depart for it is time for me to board
as i move towards the gate door i feel a tap on my shoulder
it's the young man standing there, smiling that broad smile again,
holding a folded piece of paper in his hand saying,

"here's a poem for the road"

and i read it as i walk to my seat and after i'm seated
i read it more and more and i'm pleased with the moment of sharing

BONI JOI

Brooklyn, NY Seen from Space

It's been mapped, photographed, and described many times
what you can see from the moon and what you cannot.

Each of us at our own subway stop, on a street, in our
bathroom where we hide in the shower on Tuesday nights
as the larger world continues on without us.

We look out the window, look up and wonder if
someone in the Andromeda galaxy is gazing at our Milky Way
also hiding and thinking our same exact thoughts.

With all of this life stretching out around us
will we ever be heard, will we be missed
is someone missing us right now?

JENNIFER JUNEAU

Mirror Image

From my kitchen window
I can see her.
She resides in a pane of glass.
I watch her flit across her flat
in perfectly timed succession:
first the icebox, then the oven
then she is gone.
I suppose a timer goes off
because she returns to oven
with celerity and finally
apple kuchen.
This ritual continues each day.
I know this woman well—
I imagine it is she who watches me—
she is a halcyon with steadfast eyes
and I, unaware, hovering
over the kitchen sink
elbow deep in inky blue soap.
She studies me, intrigued
by my resolution to household.
She even writes a poem about me,
evaluating my life--the callow wife.
Until one night the light
in her kitchen goes out.
I am left in the dark.
I wait.
I watch and wait
in the interior of my world
while she steps out in the exterior of hers.
Are they not the same?

QURRAT ANN KADWANI

There Are Days When the Sky Cries for Me

There are days when the sky cries for me
When memories are washed up like the dirty streets
When moments become blurred like droplets swiped on a windshield
When laughter fades, made faint with the howling wind

I let the rain blanket my sorrow
I let the rain shroud my despair
I let the rain mask my anguish

There are days when the thought of you fills me up like a river
overflowing
When I am soaked with the connection of east 88th street and Bronx Park
East
When I am drenched with the discomfort of seeing a tall man that will
never be you
When I am flooded with the fleeting rays of going shopping for that
perfect summer dress

I let the rain layer my regret
I let the rain coat my mourning
I let the rain paint my lament
There are days when your words drown me like a body submerged
When they are repeated everyday splashing me with darkness
When they sink me deeper into the dark puddles of death
When they become the reality that I didn't do enough

If you were here, I would tell you:
The clouds never go away
Even on the brightest of days, it is raining in my soul

LINDA KLEINBUB

Ode to "The Rimes Show"

Once I was a wandering poet
stumbling in and out of random dark rooms
then I entered the basement of Three of Cups Lounge.

Wrote my name on the list
sat on an empty barstool in the back of the room
downed a few cans of PBR, and watched the open mic.

When my name was called, poetry papers trembled in my hand,
my heart pounded, on stage, my voice cracked,
I was barely able to get my words
to transmit through the microphone before me.

Yet, the audience was attentive and politely applauded.
I felt welcomed, so I kept coming back
and the world continued to spin all around.

It wasn't just me, others agreed,
this "Ancient Mariner" ran a good show,
a military man, he always started on time.

He canvased other venues city-wide
searched for undiscovered talent to feature,
and he pulled it together in an artistic nurturing slurry.

Every last Wednesday of the month
poets came to share their craft
the puzzle pieces of writing life.
In this space, you could hear
a doctor who recites Seuss-like rhymes,
and see performers who burst into song.

Here you could see a grown man shout about
the joys of drunk college girls dancing
and sometimes you could hear French poetry,
that you knew was so sexy,
even if you couldn't translate a single word.

Once I was a wandering writer
rolling through the East Village
the winds of fate brought me here,
it soon became my poetic home.
Today we celebrate the Fifth Anniversary of the Rimes show
in this basement of an Italian restaurant-
a business soon closing.

Is this the last "Rimes" show?
Where will the writers go?

RON KOLM

Black Snake Moan

The Standing Rock Sioux had a bad dream. And that dream was of a big black snake, and they all knew, right away, what their dream meant. And it did not mean something good, they knew that too. The Sioux took this dream as a warning, a warning that outsiders were going to poison their water. That their water was about to be cursed. This water was Lake Oahe, and the snake was the Dakota Access Pipeline, and the blood that filled this black snake, and that made the snake evil, was oil, the life-blood still of the non-Native folks who surrounded the Cheyenne River reservation, from sea to polluted sea -- the same non-Native Americans who had taken their land so many years ago, and who continue to destroy it right up to this very day, even though everyone knows better. Because the good folks of Bismarck, North Dakota, all had dreams too, but their dreams were different – there were no snakes in their dreams, unless they were dreaming about sex. In their no dreaming life, they had pushed the black snake some distance away, because on some level even they knew that the black snake was death, and they had the power to keep it away from their water, but not so far away that they couldn't suck blood out of it from time to time – their way of life depended on it.

Many years ago, old blues musicians had sung about the black snake, but to them it was something else; it meant sex and life, not death, but the Sioux know that now it doesn't mean sex, or life, it only means that they'll get screwed.

The black snake kept slithering closer, and soldiers and police came to protect it, and the way of death in life it represented. But then other Native Americans and kind folks from all over this county arrived to keep the snake at bay, and to protect a way of life that has been disappearing for so many years, creating a stand-off. And then two thousand armed volunteers, some of them members of Black Lives Matter and some who were military vets showed up to stand shoulder to shoulder with the Standing Rock Sioux. And this gave pause to the Great Black Father who was more or less running the country, and he said let the snake go elsewhere; we can work something out. But he was replaced by a very evil huckster, who undid this great notion, and said no, I like the great black snake, let it crawl all over this land, and his tiny white snake stood up, or tried to stand up, and cheer.

PTR KOZLOWSKI

I Heard A Clock Tock When I Died

I heard a clock tock when I died
not really
for one thing I didn't die yet
and besides, I got rid of the clock that went TOCK.
I had this clock that went tock.
It was the rotary kind, with a second hand that advanced in increments
And with every step,
because of the resonance of the plastic housing in which it was mounted,
it made a sound like "TOCK".
It didn't take long to conjure in my mind the idea
that I could get another clock of similar design but of a smaller size
and it would have made the same sound but in a higher register
thus providing the missing TICK for this one's TOCK.
They could have been a perfect match like soul mates
or complements like yin and yang.
But the trouble is neither of them is calibrated to a reliable standard
and they'd just drift in and out of sync,
going from total duet harmony, to call-and-response,
and back again and around again.
Can you imagine lying awake at night with that?
With each stroke each one is trying to get ahead of the other
and the battles of Ti-tock and Tah-tick
recall a long-running argument
that persists and can't quit.
But the unaccompanied TOCK becomes evocative
of the sound made by those funny shoes that women wear
that go clock clock clock when they go walking down the block.
And there's a vast gulf between that kind of clocking
and sitting there listening to this thing going Tock - Tock -
It starts to sound like MOCK. Mock - mock - taunting me.
What? Cause I don't happen to have
any of that kind of clockwork in my life?
So wot.

I was usually always partial to the low heel types anyway.
So away with this Tock Clock Mock, I say.
Out, damned Tock!
Let's take this outside and smash it
with a rock.

WAYNE KRAL

LESwindowSHOPPING

When I drink and am enlightened
Watching one foot behind the other
Knowing home is around any corner
Passing banks, boutique money covers
Chain stores, why bother?
Snub my nose at your dis-order
Sitting next to dinosaurs
Windows covered, gates down
Mindful of anarchist robbers
Mindful of your hate for the left-overs
I miss Lenny for what he said
I miss Barbara because she's dead
I miss Mick before he danced with Taylor Swift
I want to break your window
But I gotta buy a brick

BETH CORLISS LAMONT

Hibernating Heart

Sweetheart, cold and lonely is the Winter
Enchanted Earth, beneath her blanket sleeps so still
Breezes moan laments of empty sadness
And thunder grumbles discontented on the hill

Golden Summer sky has turned to silver
And etched upon it silhouettes of naked trees
Gone are love and life and warmth and laughter
And now I huddle by my hearth of memories

Could our eternal moment be all through?
Perhaps love lies asleep to wake anew?
All alone and afraid, Oh, Sweetheart, I need you so!
Hand to hold, heart to trust. Where you are, there I must go!

Nature's trust in kindly fate leaves hope
Within my Hibernating Heart.
Dormant dreaming love awaits
The promise of a new start

Tinkling melody of sparkling water
'Neath the irreverence of skaters lies entombed
Sparrows flown, their cradle rocks abandoned
And barren branches left where lovely roses bloomed

So, lavish with our endless Summer treasure
Yet, inescapable as Winter that we part.
Sweetheart, where's your magic kiss of Springtime?
Come, wake the world and wake my Hibernating Heart

JEAN LE BEC

Butterfly Kiss
September 30, 1966

I am marrying George Miller. My High School sweetheart! We are standing under the hoopa. The ceremony is long and it's in Yiddish. We don't understand one word of it. Then finally the Rabbi says the words we've been waiting to hear. "I now pronounce you husband and wife… you may kiss Mrs. Miller." I turn to Fred, my eyes are closed, this is the kiss I have imagined. This is the kiss that every bride dreams of… and Fred turns and kisses his mother.

It was a sign!

1972 – The height of the Woman's Movement

I am 24 years old. I have two children. My daughter Aimee is 3 years old and my husband, who acts like he is 3 years old. I am getting caught up in the energy and excitement of the woman's movement. I take Aimee with me on so many demonstrations that if you say "Hello" to her, she will tell you to "burn your bra."

When New York City initiates a policy called Open Admissions where the only requirements needed to enroll in college is a HS diploma, I enroll in Brooklyn College as an education major. Hundreds of women go back to school under this initiative. Most of us left our educations behind to get married, to raise children or we didn't think we were smart enough to go to college, it just wasn't an option for us as women. Now we were learning how to redefine ourselves and going to school we knew was an important step.

None of us have childcare and so classes are filled with nursing mothers taking notes with one hand and cranky toddlers crawling under chairs. I have Aimee in a baby backpack and I kind of bounce up and down and feed her pretzels and animal crackers to keep her quiet so I can focus on the lecture. The professors are going crazy.

A small group of us form a committee and we urge the administration to give us a room in one of the buildings on campus so that we can set up some kind of daycare center. Reluctantly they do. We bring in cribs, cots, books, and toys. We make up a schedule and in between classes we run to the center to give hugs, wipe tears, read stories, make lunches. Women students who are not moms find their way to our daycare center. We become more than a daycare center. The center becomes a place where women can meet and talk and share.

Mid-year, the administration decided to take the room away. So early on a very cold January morning, about ten of us tucked pillows under our clothing pretending to be pregnant and marched around with signs chanting… "We've been fucked by the administration."

By noon, at least 100 women have tucked pillows under their clothing and are holding signs chanting we've been fucked by the administration. More and more students leave their classes and join our demonstration. The police are called. Bystanders yell at us, "Go home, feed your husbands, and take care of your kids."

We are a powerful force and the administration gives us our room. This room grows into two rooms and then three rooms. The agency for Child Development funds us and we officially become The Brooklyn College Daycare Center, the first daycare center on a NYC college campus. Women are trading their make-up, sexy black dresses, and high heels for white T-shirts, overalls, and beige work boots. We go to Women's Consciousness Groups.

My friend Sally has organized one and every Wednesday evening we sit cross-legged on the burnt orange shag rug in her living room. We share a joint, laugh, and cry. We confess our sins. We give advice.

A woman might share… "My husband wants me to put on a dress and wear something sexy!"

Advice: "Leave him!"

A woman might share… "My husband doesn't want to just cuddle; he always wants sex!"

Advice: "Leave him!"

There should have been a sign on the door, "If you enter this room in a relationship with a man you will leave without that man unless that man is your son."

The book *Our Bodies, Ourselves* had just come out and we read passages out loud to each other like it was some kind of sex novel.

It was at one of these meetings that I meet Mona. I like her right away. She has shiny auburn hair to her shoulders and grey-green eyes. She has such style. Her overalls are embroidered with tiny red and yellow flowers on green zig zagging vines. She smokes Benson & Hedges and she has this way of inhaling and saying, "That's just Bullshit" as she exhales. I just love the way she says, "That's just Bullshit."

After 6 months in Sally's woman's group my marriage ends and so does Mona's. We become friends. Her daughter Ingrid is exactly the same age as my daughter Aimee. We live just a few blocks away from each other in Park Slope. We begin to rely on each other. If I need help with Aimee she is there and if she needs help with Ingrid I am there. We begin to cook dinner together and do laundry together… a natural rhythm forms. We laugh constantly and when I'm not with her, there is always something that I just can't wait to tell her.

We have one major disagreement and that is what we call our vaginas. Aimee and I call our vaginas a vagina. Mona just hates the word Vagina. Ingrid and Mona call their vaginas a snatch, which totally drives me crazy. We decide to change the names of the vaginas and we decide on Pussy. But the girls can't make the transition so now Aimee is calling her vagina my vagina pussy and Ingrid is calling her vagina my snatch pussy. It's like the vaginas now have two names.

One evening we get babysitters and we go to see the movie *Cabaret*. After the movie, we are sitting in Mona's car, right outside my apartment building. We are talking about the movie and singing one of the songs… "Money makes the world go round, the world go round."

Suddenly Mona stops singing and looks at me and says, "I really feel like kissing you." I laugh… "so kiss me," I say, never expecting her to really kiss me.

And Mona kisses me and our lips melt. And I have never felt lips so soft. I feel as though I have waited my whole life for this kiss. This was the kiss I have been waiting for. There are butterflies in my mouth and my heart is beating so loud I can hear it, and I run out of the car and into my apartment. I pace the kitchen floor. Does she feel the same way? Call me! Call me!

The phone rings and I grab it.

"Mona," I say laughing into the phone.

"Jean," Mona says laughing into the phone.

And we are both laughing and I slide down my kitchen wall gripping the phone and laughing, landing on the hard-cold linoleum knees to chin holding the phone and laughing.

So, we became lovers but we really didn't know what to do without a penis. If you can imagine tiny little kittens kind of rolling around each other licking and nipping … that was what we were doing.
One evening, the girls weren't home; Mona lit candles. She put on Carol King and to the song, "You've Got A Friend," Mona went past my pussy snatch vagina to this whole other place and I came… like really came… for the very first time in my life!
Before going to sleep, Mona whispered, "You know sweetie– you can do this to yourself anytime you want to."

Well, I woke up that morning with this newfound power. I worked at a daycare center about 6 blocks from my house and I had a 45-minute lunch period. Every day, the moment it was lunch, I would run those 6 blocks, pray that the elevator didn't get stuck on some godforsaken floor and I masturbated. I masturbated on my bed without clothes, with clothes, at my kitchen table, in front of a mirror.

Then one lunchtime, just as I was about to leave, I am confronted by 4 of my co-workers. Pauline says, "You are not going anywhere!" They surround me and I am ushered into an empty classroom. We are sitting in a semi-circle. Pauline, the spokesperson for the group says, "Where are you going every day? You never eat lunch with us anymore. The moment its lunch you run out of here… you missed Neil's birthday. And you come back from lunch looking really weird. Are you mad at us?"
"No … no … I'm not mad at all … I'm masturbating"

Pauline just looks at me and I can't really believe that I just said that and she says, "Everyday?"
"Yup, everyday but listen, tomorrow it stops and I'm eating lunch with you."
Pauline is quiet for a moment and then she says, "No… tomorrow I'm going home and I'm masturbating."

Mona and I were together for five years when she told me that she was moving to Maine. I wasn't surprised. Mona spent summers building a cabin on land her family-owned and she always dreamed of living off the land. She wanted Aimee and me to go with her but it wasn't my dream.

The first two years, we wrote passionate love letters, our phone calls ended in tears, visits with anguished good-byes.
And then we started to melt away from each other. We let each other go and suddenly 45 years passed without a word.
I found her on Facebook. We made a telephone date. I was so nervous calling her. And then there she was.
"Mona," I said.
"Jean," Mona said.
And we started laughing.
For one moment, I was once more that very young woman sliding down her kitchen wall, holding a butterfly kiss and she was wearing embroidered overalls.

JANE LECROY

Dying Wishes

He's holding a beer, in most every memory I have of him
my childhood cluttered with glass bottles, multiplying, metastasizing
after decades of alcohol and cocaine, he was 14 years clean
but only morphine could relieve the pain—stage four at 54—pancreatic
cancer, he needed too much dope to die at home, so he was admitted
into hospice where kindly, retired, firemen strolled the halls, pushing
a cart of top-shelf liquor and everything besides, to comfort
the dying and those who love them: vodka, whiskey, wine, gin
and even Pabst Blue Ribbon, his old staple, the piss
draining from his body through a tube, was the color of Guinness
now during his last nights on Earth, I encouraged him to have a drink,
he had enjoyed it so much once upon a time, "No," he said,
as the IV drip trickled from above his bed, machine blinking MORPHINE
over his head, "I'm dying sober."

LINDA LERNER

Apple Picking Kisses
(after reading *Kiss Hierarchy* by Alexandra Van De Kamp on my upcoming birthday)

August stalls in September. What can I do?
Nothing moves. Half lit, yellowing stale like cigarettes
from a Bogart film I want to stamp out, one day
after the next left to extinguish themselves and don't;
my cat stretched out beside me on the couch, his
green eyes opening just long enough to breeze in a grassy
bird flying place with tiny figures whose faces I can't
make out busy filling up baskets and mouths with
27 apples and kisses falling out of the sky and close
before I can reach out to grab one; what's the point?
I lie back imagining Seurat painting a cool apple
falling September day for me with kisses breaking out
of apples and a 1940's leading male actor, a cigarette
dangling from his mouth, you know the one,
coming toward me through a smoky haze

KAREN LEVY

Fury

The raft was made of a soft mesh that allowed her body to dip into the water. It was nothing like the rafts and tubes the vendors sold on the beach, those fluorescent plastics that propped you up so that you lay atop, hot and sticky. Even as the Sunday crowds played noisily in the shallow waters of Boca Chica, throwing bottles of rum and yelling and splashing and making out, Serena was lulled to sleep, enveloped by the sea. Her bikini showed the smooth, tight, hugeness of her belly.

Yahaira stood beside her with one hand on the raft. Colorless fish encircled her waist. They were good friends now, best friends, except that Serena wouldn't share the secret behind the hugeness of her belly. She went red when Yahaira asked; shook her head and pressed her lips closed. Yahaira knew it was shame for what she'd done, but she would have the baby anyway.

A group of pelicans soared overhead. Without warning, they dove into the waters quite close to the bathers, surfacing with large silver-bellied fish in their bills. Flapping along the surface of the water, they swallowed their prey and rose up to search out their next bite. As they circled overhead, the bathers were caught in the excitement of the hunt, with some children screaming in terror at becoming the birds' delight.

"Serena!" Yahaira shook the raft. "I'm going for Papi's camera. I have to get a picture of these birds. I'll be right back."

The games of tossing bottles of rum and building pyramids stopped as everyone watched the precision with which half a dozen birds hit the water and rose with their beaks full. One pelican rose from the sea with an enormous fish in its beak. It struggled with its prey as it flew higher and higher, and it seemed that all the bathers caught their breath when they saw that fish. It was bigger than the bird itself, big enough to feed a family.

The fish, a deep red color, fought back. It shook itself partway out of the giant bill, but the bird gulped at it over and over to prevent its escape. The bathers laughed and cheered and made bets on both sides.

"I'm going with the bird."

"I'll put fifty on the fish."

"One more wiggle, baby!"

"He can't escape. That bill is the biggest I've seen!"

A second bird flew in. It tried to snatch the giant prey, but the first bird swallowed down the better part of the fish, and then struck his opponent with the fish's head. The bathers roared with delight. The second bird flew off screaming but returned to fly circles around the first. Then it lunged.

The first bird veered sharply, struggling as it rose higher and higher above the water's surface to escape the attack. Its wings beat powerfully as it moved vertically with its prey, but then it opened its beak just the slightest bit, just enough for the fish to twist away and free fall the great distance back to the sea. Its scaled body caught the sun and shone iridescent as it dove toward home. Just before it hit the water, the second bird swooped in and smoothly swallowed it halfway down its enormous neck. The bathers cheered.

The fury of the fish, struggling to slip back into the sea, prevented the second bird from rising. It skimmed the ocean's surface, awkward and heavy, as all eyes watched. Its feet dragged the water, making patterns of wakes and gentle waves. Then, with a long stretch of its neck, it swallowed down even more of the giant fish, whose head created an obscene bulge in the bird's long neck. The bathers clapped their hands and traded dirty jokes as the bird flapped frantically and then rose from the water to fly off.

No one noticed the sleeping woman floating away. Once Serena drifted from the circle of bathers, she was caught in a current that quickly pulled her out from the safety of the beach into the open sea. She was just a speck of white belly when Yahaira returned for her.

"Papi! Papi!" she shouted for her father, "It's Serena!"

He stood up from his chair and followed her finger as she pointed out to sea.

"She's floating away!" Yahaira yelled, and they both ran for one of the fishing boats on shore.

"Llama la policia!" Call the police! He shouted at a man with a phone. *"Mi mujer esta alejando hacia lo ondo!"* - My woman is floating away.

Yahaira stopped and stared at his choice of words.

The speck of white belly disappeared behind *la Matica*, the mangrove island a quarter mile out that separated them from the sea.

He yelled for her help and they pushed the boat through the crowds of Sunday bathers. People jumped out of their way. They climbed in. Her father pulled the oars out from under the seat and rowed wildly.

All the while, Yahaira stayed calm. She'd been quick to react, running for her father and heaving the boat into the waist-deep waters to save her friend. Now, she was stilled by his frenzy.

He was speaking to himself, fast and low under his breath, "Oh, God! Help me! Why isn't there a motor? *Coño!*" as he plunged the oars into the water.

She didn't offer to help - she just watched him lose himself to his rescue attempt.

"How is this happening?"

He dropped an oar and had to jump overboard for it. The sun played tricks on them. They traveled in circles.

Finally, they reached the raft; it was running its own course. Serena was gone.

Her father threw down the oars. *"Coño! Que vaina!"* Tears fell from his eyes like stones: hard and round; they bounced off his thighs and over the hull of the boat, into the sea.

He stood up and jumped. Yahaira sat back; cold to his loss. He dove down into the dark blue water, resurfaced and dove again. She lost count of how many times. He dove until he was exhausted. Bobbing with one hand on the boat's hull, he sucked in huge mouthfuls of air.

"*La Policia!*" came a shout from a motorboat headed their way.

"*Ayudame!* Help!" Her father croaked between ragged breaths. "*Coño!* She's pregnant with my baby!"

Yahaira threw up into the beautiful, salty sea.

MARIA LISELLA

The Urban Disappeared

Acrid smells: acid, steel,
Burnt wires
Crisp black carbon on an iron pan.

Whites of eyes shown red
Throats lined with pulverized steel, bone.

Ghosts walk among us:
Living inside the living
Walking forever wounded.

They march in perfect step at rush hours
Up and down Broadway, Church Street
East on Fulton, up the steps of St. Paul's.

They stand on lines at coffee carts
Keep time-worn routines at appointed hours.
Silent, invisible, in day, in night.

The urban disappeared float
In and out of twin tower cavities
A cosmos of thick visible air
No longer served by elevators.

Sip steaming coffee at desks.
Clouds rise above lips
Stare into sky in space.

Mouths open to call spouses,
No one hears them.
Peer into photos on desks.
Seek exit, escape, egress
Infinite frames replay Sept. 11
Stuttering into the 21st century.

MIKE LOGAN

Czech Republic(e)

Can a stripper from the Czech Republic be legally entitled to the status of my "girlfriend"? If so, then I'm fucking around behind my topless dancer "girlfriend's" back. I sacrificed my neighbor's little black toy poodle, Fifi, to the chief Teutonic god, Wotan, praying for the Valhalla Almighty to send me a new girlfriend.

Don't worry; my dog-loving neighbor is a Satanist, so she'll understand.

Just don't say anything about it to her.

Then Freya, the pagan love goddess, sent me a ninety-nine-pound anorexia nervosa Eastern European stripper, with no tits and a big fat ass, better known as Gigi, the girl of my dreams. She resembles a twelve-year-old pre-pubescent Catholic schoolgirl. Again, don't worry; she's 25 years old. I checked out her passport and Student Visa. She's studying business at NYU, working her way through college giving lap dances and hand jobs in the VIP Champagne Room of New York Dolls strip club in Tribeca. She's got ambitions for a better life.

So, tonight, I'll go to their "sister" strip club FlashDance in Midtown just to avoid running into Gigi.

I'm "cheating" on her with a transgender, Thai, topless dancer who has a huge setta fake silicone tits and the tiny, soft behind of a ten-year-old boy. Not that I would ever know what a ten-year-old boy's Heine feels like. I'm just saying.

Just don't say anything to Gigi if you see her.

Why? Why do I "cheat" on Gigi? I suppose, even amongst strippers, variety is the spice of life? I fucked around behind the back of each of my previous four ex-wives so why should "now" be different? Do I owe "monogamy", "fidelity", to a sex worker?

I never told Gigi to quit her job blowing out of town businessmen in the high-end Sapphire Room of New York Dolls. I don't judge her. Why should she judge me?

Butt…

Having dated strippers, porn stars, dominatrices, escorts, call girls, "happy ending" massage parlor "masseuses", go-go dancers and burlesque queens, I have painfully discovered that these "sex workers" are just as inclined, if not more so, to be insanely jealous of any "extra-marital" affairs. They demand absolute fidelity, I suppose because they are exposed to men who are blatantly cheating… on a wife, or a girlfriend… with them.

"I'm a Gemini. That's why I'm so jealous." Dee, the escort/erotic massager/porn star, confronted me with after she caught me merely "dirty dancing" with some female poet. Suffice it to say, our "relationship" did not survive.

So. If you run into Gigi sometime and she starts asking you a buncha questions about me… Like, where was I?… What was I doing?… Or who was I doing it with?… Just tell her I was with YOU!

MICHAEL LYDON

BB King in the Deep South

The sun sank in the west as the bus rolled by mile after mile of darkening sugar cane fields. At Baton Rouge a cab driver gave me a hard stare when I said I wanted to go the Club Streamline across the Mississippi in Port Allen, then he spit on the ground and waved me into his cab. After crossing a high bridge over the slow rolling river, we pulled off into a graveled parking lot before a low, long cinderblock building. A neon sign flickered, *Club Streamline*. The driver screeched to a halt. I paid my fare, got out, and he was gone.

By now it was full night. I entered under a ripped green and white awning, paid my cover charge, and walked in, the only white person in the club. I found Frank, BB's driver and my contact man. "Glad you made it," he said, "BB's going on in a minute, come see him at the break." I took a seat in the back. The crowd—field workers in collarless shirts, city dudes over from Baton Rouge, orange-haired beauticians, refinery workers with their wives—sat around chipped linoleum top tables, drinking, laughing, talking, shouting, and flirting, and paying me no mind at all.

"We want BB!" shouted a woman with a heavy sprinkling of gold teeth. "Deed we do," answered her mousy friend, but the five-piece band kept running through "Eleanor Rigby."

From a side door, a valet carried in a red electric guitar, plugged it into a silver-fronted amplifier and left it gleaming on a chair. "If Lucille's here, BB can't be far behind," said the gold-tooth lady. The sax player grabbed a microphone. "Ladies and gentlemen, it's *show* time and we're *hap*py to pre*sent* the *star* of the show, the *King* of the Blues, *Mr. B, B, King!*" A wave of clapping washed back to the bar as a heavy-set man in a shiny maroon suit stepped lightly to the stage and picked up the guitar. The band started a swinging blues, and BB, eyes, screwed shut and body bent forward, hit a quick chord. The club roared its approval.

"From that instant," I wrote, "the very molecules of the air seemed alive, King's guitar becoming a magic source of energy that drew the whole club into its tremulous, hesitant intensity." I'd been to the Apollo and jazz and

R&B clubs all through college, and I'd been to Negro churches and honky-tonks in Mississippi in '64, but I'd never felt so immersed in the black world as I did that September night at the Club Streamline. These were black folks out from under white eyes, and they were having one hell of a good time.

On the first break, I found my way backstage. BB gave me a warm welcome, then went back to work. Midnight came and went. BB and the band played set after set, fast blues, slow blues, BB's guitar and barrel-chested voice showing the way. Gradually the tables emptied. Two-thirty: time to pack up. The promoter, with a guilty look, said he didn't have all the money promised, would BB take $200 less? BB didn't like it, but what could he do? He took the offered envelope, and Frank put in a bulging leather briefcase.

We left the club at 3 am, me riding with BB in the green Fleetwood Cadillac, the band packed into a Ford Econovan. The plan: drive two hundred miles to a motel in Mobile, sleep through the day, then set out for Montgomery. While gassing up in Baton Rouge, three guys in the band, all wearing dashikis and all from the North, headed to the café across the parking lot for sandwiches; I went with them. We sat down on stools. No eating at the counter, said the doorman, no takeouts either. A dozen white toughs watched over their beers. With a look between us, we decided to retreat. "We're Wallaces," shouted a tough. "Good for you," BB's bass player sneered going out the door. "Whah, you nigger," said a tough, coming out after him and punching him to the gravel. "Git 'em," cried another tough, and suddenly the whites were outside, one swinging a heavy chain.

I ran back to the relative safety of the brightly lit gas station, but the three fought back. When Frank, a giant, came running and grabbed away the chain, the whites scattered. Tenor saxist Lee Gatling had been stabbed in the arm and trumpeter Pat Williams was bleeding from a chain wound on his forehead. Off in the men's room, BB had missed the action, but he quickly took charge, ordering an ambulance, calming his men, and talking to the police, who, after asking a few questions, said they could find no suspects.

Once the cops left, the tension began to melt. The fellows ribbed me plenty about my precipitous flight; all I could do was blush and say I'd been scared to death. "Just when you think things are getting better," said BB to no one in particular, staring at the "I Have a Dream" stickers on his bumper. "Man, this hurts so bad. And they tease me for singing the blues. Hah! What else can I sing?"

We waited at a little Negro hospital until six am before a doctor Okayed Williams to travel. As the sun rose, we started for Mobile, getting there, sleepless in the glare of early afternoon.

Riding that evening to Montgomery BB and I sat in the leather backseat of the sleek green Cadillac, Frank silent at the wheel. BB told me his life story, going back to his mother dying when he was a child, how he chopped cotton on a plantation, joined a gospel group but snuck off to play blues, "the devil's music," on street corners in Jackson and Oxford; how success on Memphis radio led to his first hit, "Three O'Clock Blues," in '49 that launched a chitlin' circuit career which had continued, 340 one-nighters a year, for most of twenty years. BB told his tale modestly, but just below the surface of this handsome, intelligent forty-year-old burned a driving ambition to sing and play and tell his story, not just to the black world, but to the whole world. "If Frank Sinatra can be tops in his field," he said more than once, "Nat Cole in his, Bach and Beethoven and those guys in theirs, why can't I be known as great in the blues? I'm not saying the rockers don't deserve their fame, but think I deserve mine too."

That night a good-time crowd packed the Montgomery Elk's Club, Southern Pride Lodge No. 431, to the walls, and BB worked them like a master, his face beaded with sweat, his guitar Lucille high up under his chin, his eyebrows arching and falling, his voice one moment bellowing, one moment cooing, and the people swaying, oohing, laughing, and clapping at his command. I watched and listened from table by the kitchen transfixed. Damn! This is what music can do!! God, to sing and play like that, get that response, that would be the greatest fun on earth!

On a break the fellows talked about last night's fight the night. "Nothing like that ever happened to me," said Pat Williams, "You ever see anything like that, B?"

"No," said BB, "but when I started out, I didn't stay in Holiday Inns, I kept food in the car, and relieved myself by the side of the road. My only regret about last night is, you fellas didn't put one of them in the hospital."

"Next time," said Pat.

Through my last day we rolled east to the Livonia Country Club, a shack at the end of a dirt road maze twenty miles from Atlanta. The Livionia was the pits: bare wooden chairs and tables, cracked cement floor, and a stage lined with tin foil, lit by one fixed spotlight. I'd heard Apollo comedians joke about a "wish sandwich"— "How do you make a wish sandwich? Jes' put two slices of bread together 'n wish you had some meat!"—but thought the sandwich was mythical until that night at the Livonia where the hand-written menu offered a "Sandwich Plain": two slices of white bread with a thin coating of mayonnaise in between.

The small crowd refused to clap. "You know we're working hard for you," BB pleaded, "whyncha beat your hands together for us?" but he got only scattered applause. He played roughly, slashing his pick across harshly vibrant chords, even breaking two strings. "Worry, worry, worry," he sang, "My life is so miserable, baby, and it's all on account of you."

Then, like all shows good or bad, it ended. "Thank you, thank you," BB shouted leaving the stage. He thanked the band for playing well, changed his clothes, and got into the Fleetwood. Frank steered the car back through the dirt road maze to the highway. BB turned on the portable television he kept plugged into the cigarette lighter; a black and white gangster movie was playing.

"What's happening? He asked Frank.

"Another day done passed by," said Frank.

JENNA LYNCH

With Your Eyes Alone

You lick the tip of a cigarette, push the tobacco against the sting,
hold it against your head while he looks for a poem.

Reception for first year graduate students,

everyone pretending to be interested,
pretending to hear what the other is saying, holding

tightly to plastic cups as they circle the room. He's ready to leave,
but you want to stick around a while,

inhabit another self for an hour or two,
your mouth a gaping hole of hysterics, and hands that hurt.

Lately everyone is giving you advice to "take it easy"
when you could be coming from behind,

your hair pulled back, his pierced cock with prince's wand, neck bites,
memories of those mornings of early consciousness—
Ginsberg's key in the window, letters from his mother urging
        marriage, clean living,

            her wishing strongly he was someone else,

her with *the long black beard around the vagina.*

Instead you want to know everything, even what doesn't matter:

oxblood colored trousers, black spike heel booties, removable collars
in the copy of Vogue, Fall issue, the one with Keira Knightley on the
cover,

hair piece that makes a kind of shield—

       all things worth knowing,

like his hands now, thumb and index making a steeple on his chin.

The girl behind you asks,   "can I have a sip of water," then,
"aren't you listening?"

But you're thinking of something else, you forget to answer, close your
eyes
for a second to catch your breath.

And you know now things will never be easy:
you look in a mirror and see   mother, brother, twin,
shadow, skeleton—

you are anything you want,

     even a little boy.

You light the cigarette backwards, with a hand shading your face,

with a face like hers,

with his face open, talking.

TAYLOR MALI

To Better See the Letters of Your Name

Your grandson brushed pine needles from your name in the woods,
from the carved stone marker where we buried your ashes.
A grandson you never met, which is all of them,
so let me rather say by my son. I have a son named after you.

Which might be why he cried all night and hardly slept,
or why he swept the granite marker clear, to better see
the letters of your name, or do the math of missing you,
how many years. He's quiet now. His tears like you are gone.

At your grave this morning in this stand of pine,
between the old stone wall and abandoned railroad track,
your grandson cleared your name of needles with his hands.
And then, before we left, he put them back.

PETER MARRA

Forgotten Incidents: A Bad Friend, A Good Crucifixion.

Blood Moon Bang-Bang.
(a Face) the Sweet Body
in recent years, the hands in these gestures were arising from the streets to
the stations of our cross. we're bleeding. a holy moisture for our forgotten
prey. the mischief of a touch, a lick of the lips instead of our prayers. it
contorted with the pleasure and lightly tongued the window pane. the
creature could not be defined by standard scientific exploratory
techniques, so the cage door was left open – for it to escape.

evolution:
for us to forget it existed. opening scene: Duomo Square Florence.
violinists (she appears in the back). olive skin long black hair tattered
dress. she glides without movement. transfiguration. a video undergoing
experimental climaxes manipulated
by vacant stares. we're never going to leave this place are we? this skin of
stucco, this void that throbs. the moon spins left whenever she enters the
room, passing from one room to another, clasping a random heart in her
left hand.

making a *mano fico* with her right paw. she wears a vest of horsehair and
nothing else. her sex is on display. inconsequential meanderings brought
her to this present state. not satiated. singing gentle songs right before the
ritual starts. the slender female strangers mouth words of unknown origin
as they walk cobblestone streets. coarse words from their fathers' corpses
eternal high contrast black and white burns up the monitor.

play it backwards and tell me what you see
play it backwards and tell me what you hear. just tell me what you fear.

listen: the conversations of females: "night has an envelope waiting for
me. a seclusion so strange yet comforting in its liquidity. a carrier of tiny
flesh scratches while titillating the evening sky. loneliness cured by a
black box waiting for us to enter."

say prayers to Madonna Tenebrae jude in plain sight, eyes turned inwards to admire the footprints. wandering helter skelter, she caressed the vintage movie box before

licking her only window. they scream sans vocal cords - a mutation of what had really occurred in the past: the never-spoken, the never-seen and the babble.

the wandering feminine mirrors clutched a broken face close to their hearts. the pupae stole the faces of the wife and reclaimed them for its own. she professed her love of cocoons. the echolocating of lunar moths intrigued these women. the direction of light during the totemic ceremonies gave them no satisfaction. another came in for the kill.

C. O. MOED

Last Night

It was the usual fistfight
my older sister punching my mother as hard as she was getting punched

And I don't know how it all got started, I was sitting on my bed
Which is where I usually sit when I watch people beating the fuck out of
one another
as if each punch was the road to being loved or being heard or being
whatever

When suddenly my mother got wild, got wild I don't know how she could
have pushed my sister
even deeper into the corner of the bed but she did and I watched her grab
my sister's head and begin

Bashing it, bashing it uncontrollably against the wall uncontrollably over
and over and over and over and…

Like she had exploded at a billion miles an hour into a monster with no
brain ravenous and tearing apart

And my father who never intervened…
because fistfights made him crippled again, his wife filling up with the
ghost of his father, the Ox-there was no winning when the Ox pummeled
them into the wall- my father went and married the ghost of the Ox and
even if she was beautiful and even if he did love her so much and even if
she did love him maybe, he could never stop her even when he was still
hitting her or hitting her back until one day he just decided to stop hitting
everyone

And my father who never intervened
ran into our small bedroom where I was sitting on my bed as I always did
when people were beating the fuck out of one another and I watched him
for the first time pull the ghost of his father off his daughter

Who sobbed, who sobbed uncontrollably
Because even though her father loved her she only loved the woman who
was beating the fuck out of her

I don't remember for sure but I think I did something for the first time
I took my wool poncho and I closed the front door behind me
Maybe I was 12, perhaps I was 13, it was definitely winter and I walked to
Essex and Grand, got on the Avenue A bus, the driver let me smoke his
cigarettes and we traveled uptown in the middle of the night talking about
family

He let me off at St. Marks and I walked maybe for the first time but
definitely not the last
into brutal cold looking for home and a break from monsters

Twenty years later watching Jurassic Park in a movie theater, I would
panic terror that had nothing to do with dinosaurs

And twenty years after Jurassic Park I would ask my sister about that night
And she would say she didn't remember

ANTHONY MOSCINI

R e

s   c

m   t

u

Yes Sometimes known as assholes
are an important part of any day   Yeah

They everywhere move   Groovy in
a groove Sweetly passive   Little to say

Mouse/house quite Hidden shyly from
the world's probing eyes   Yet if we saw a

million I say a million in a row Spreading
Yes spreading rose garlands about them

t'would be a way to give or show The
earth's a place to come then go   Yet how

Oh how do we save our sacred souls on
a planet with so many assholes

ANTHONY C. MURPHY

Mum

There is a list up there with the names of all those to appear in front of the magistrates this day. I see my name, somewhere in the middle of the morning. At least I am not first, that would have made me paranoid as all hell. Then I hear my name. It shocks me.

"Hello, Sean!"

It's my mum. She's looking older, tired, but it's definitely her.

"Fuck me, Mum! What are you doing here?"

"SEAN!" She hits me on the head. "Watch your mouth."

"Get off." I say. "It's just… how did you know?"

"You have a next of kin you know."

"What?" I can't believe that. I have no privacy. "You gave me a right shock." I say. "Come on, let's sit down." We go and find some room on a wooden bench and wait.

"So how have you been? How is the place?" Mum asks. She attempts to smooth my hair again.

"It's okay. There're guys from all over the place. Scousers, Brummies, Geordies, Jocks."

"God. We must live in the crime capital of Britain. There can't be anything left to steal, is there?"

"They're not all fuckin' thieves, Mum!"

"Language, Sean! You're spending too much time with them already. It's rubbing off." I laugh at that.

"I don't have much fucking choice." I say. She taps me on the head again. "Sorry!" I say.

"Ssssh! Will you?" She says. "What have they all done then, if they're not thieves?"

"I dunno… Something, I guess." I start talking in urgent whispers. She's made me aware of others' eavesdropping, those others waiting here, hungry for gossip and scandal in the courthouse. We straighten ourselves on the bench.

"*Something* is right. And what about you? I thought I taught you the difference between right and wrong." She's whispering too now. I think she is about to lick a tissue and apply it to me.

"Yeah…I just. I didn't… I was stuck." I say, and shrink away from her. "Don't Mum!"

"That's weak," she says, putting away her hanky.

"Well you didn't want to help," I say. She takes a gulp of air.

"There's no way I was paying for *his* funeral. Not after what he did." She says.

"I guess not." I say. I remember what he did. I remember her bruises, and her going out with sunglasses on, in Rochdale. No one wears sunglasses in Rochdale. Not only because it's always cloudy, but because it looks like you're a poser if you do. There's nothing worse in that town, on our street, than being called a poser. I also remember Joe had said that wasn't all there was to it though, the black eye.

"What did he do?" I ask playing dumb. "None of us ever talked about it. He was just gone."

He never told you? When he came back? When you were all pally and working together?" She huffs.

"No." I don't let on that he told me he wasn't the only one to blame.

"Well, you were too young," she says.

"I was sixteen."

"Still… Too young to …" She twitches. I don't know if she's twitching for a fag, but she catches herself and stops twitching.

"I'm not now though." I say. "I'm old enough to have my own place."

"Well we thought so. You proved us wrong there, didn't you?" She rubs my head. "So maybe you are still too young." She says. "Anyway, it doesn't matter now he's dead."

May the void never be so succinct with me, I think. But I don't voice it. I am an ignoramus. I shouldn't want to know. I shouldn't, but I do.

"Maybe it matters to me, Mum," I say.

She looks me in the eye then. She has green eyes and they are youthful, full of light. I see myself in them. They are so familiar to me I would never have to see them again yet I would know them in my sleep. And they smile at me. I would say they are full of love but I know better than to believe such things. I have seen them go just as glittery with meanness as Joe's eyes used to whenever, well whenever they wanted to, but usually when I had been acting selfishly. I can see in her eyes that I am a disappointment, she rolls them and they cloud and change, unlike the weather here, quickly, without warning. They are even tearing up a little.

"Okay, Seany. If I tell you, some of it, will you drop it? I don't want to think about any of it anymore." She says.

"Okay." I say.

"Okay," she says. And she sits up and takes a breath and fiddles with her handbag. "Okay," she says again, "we'd been at the Entwistle, drinking with Vinny and Sheila, singing those old Irish songs up on our feet. You were staying over at your mate's house. Do you still see Dickie?"

"No," I say. "Not much chance anyway, living where I do."

"No," she says. "I guess not. He doesn't visit?"

"Why would he?" I ask. "Go on."

"Yeah. So, it was the usual at the Entwistle Arms, but I could see Joe, your dad, was flirting, and god knows, I was at the end of my tether with that. With all of it. The animals he used to bring home. The pub every day. The betting on the horses. He spent more time at the bookies than he did at home and more time in the pub than either. At least he'd had a decent job before. When that place shut down, and he had to get temporary work, it started getting worse. It was like he didn't care anymore. Not that he ever did, I don't think, not really. We had fun sometimes. And he enjoyed you until you turned two years old and became a single-minded whirlwind. There were times though." She stopped. I wanted to hear about those times. I thought I could remember good times. Maybe one day I would. I had snatches of memory that had laughter in them. And not just that hard braying sarcastic laughter.

"Go on," I say.

"There was one time," Mum says, and she starts to cry, here in the courthouse waiting room, "when you came into our room, because you, Sean, had heard something, you must have been about three, and we were having sex, you know, sorry! But he, Joe, your dad, was so angry at the interruption. You were just saying 'Mum'. We must have woke you… He got up and hit you so hard that you flew off your feet." She had to breathe. "I should have done something then… I left it for years… but I always remembered the look on your face, not angry, just so… disappointed or something… you got up and walked away to your bedroom." She had to breathe again. "You changed from a child that night. You never wanted to come into our bed after that."

"Yeah." I say. "Was that it though?" I don't know what else to say. It's not what I want to know. "Have you got any smokes, Mum?" I ask. I can't make her feel any better. She wipes her face with a tissue from her handbag.

"Only menthol." She says. I have to think about now. So, we go outside again. I tear the filter off the cigarette and light it on the steps, and I smoke like it's my last dramatic fag. "What are you doing?" She starts to ask. There are many people out here, arguing, most of them. I see a big skinhead, and he sees me. I hope it's his third act and he gets sent down but I don't even know his first act. I see the difference between guys in suits placating these other guys out here, and some, but not many, girls they represent, those looking out of place in buttoned up shirts with tattoos peeking out, who have nothing much else but loud voices about how unlucky they are and, "Do something about it!" shouts. The whole thing makes me sick. This is all a joke I have become a part of. I look at the pub opposite, but I don't want to go there.

"What did your solicitor say, Sean?" Mum asks.

"Nothing," I say. "He's not even here yet."

"Let's go back in." She says.

She puts her arm around me and when we are back through security, and down on a wooden bench, waiting, I ask again, "Was that it though?" and we start whispering again.

"No," she says. "I knew what he was like. So, I got him to do it to me. I got him to hit me, to finish it." She gets another hanky out.

"What do you mean?" I say.

"That night, after years of it. Something happened in my head, maybe I was getting older, and you too, but when I saw him flirting and with all those others, some of them he knew, he knew more than he let on he knew. I played him on that night. I got him home, told him we would do it, and then I refused him. He couldn't handle it. He went mental. I knew he would. He hit me when I said 'No!' and I took it. I took it. I took the hits just to get rid of him. I knew that he wouldn't last here if I looked like that in the morning."

"Oh." Is all I say.

"And all the neighbors wanting a butty and a natter. I don't want a butty and a natter! The last thing I want is a butty and a natter with Sheila, who your dad was probably... you know..."

"Shagging?" I ask.

"Yes. Shagging. Thank you. I don't know why Vinny ever even tried pulling him out of the canal." She says sobbing.

"It didn't make any difference. In the end. But he did, though." I say and I pull her towards me.

"No. No. I guess not," she sobs. "Good riddance!" Mum says.

"Well," I say. "Maybe." And then my name is called by the court so I have to appear up front through the wooden door. I give my mum a kiss, I get her to sit, and I walk in to face the magistrates.

ARTHUR NERSESIAN

Secret Sacrifices

Notice all the scars,
all the scabs,
all the thick metal plates,
covering copious gaps
where the city's reproductive organs
are severed under a nightly coven
when the pavement's epiderm is peeled back.
Hoses, pipes, smokestacks,
release steam, trickle boiling water
sterilizing these sacred sites.
Every street has cuts and gashes.
They aren't all potholes
and busted water mains.
Fierce, behind each
little yellow tent encampment
is late-hour manhole surgery
-- a routine infant sacrifice.
For unspeakable horrors
and unthinkable shame,
up from countless subterranean city agencies
boil endless occult malignancies
that none can or shall ever name.

KURT NELSON PELOQUIN

Our Snakes

When I was 7 years old, I loved to venture into the sloping woods behind
our home along Maple Avenue.
Just past the line where my father, Paul, decided the grass wouldn't grow
and instead let nature take hold.
Who showed her magic dark soil of black stones, nestled wild weeds with
copper flowers, and giant trees made pillars of light forty feet tall.
We—my brother Erik and sister Grace—set off one day through the ash of
morning, scouring for some buried treasure, some X marks the spot.
Swinging branches in hand, wild reckless children, we came a thin-black-
stick. That quickly slid-black-scales. *YELLED! SWUNG-STICK-AND-
MISSED-AND-HIT-GRACE-ABOVE-HER-EYES!*
I just missed her eyes. Eyes that now save lives, but shocked then and
only five, she did not cry.
But, I've been afraid of snakes ever since.
Anything that can sneak up on you—like a habit, or a story, or a sadness—
hiding under dead skin hoping no-one will notice just how naked we are
behind these beautiful scales and strike us down, doomed.
Because deadwood splinters splay and we work jobs that don't pay; swipe
right to get laid; like, fight, and parade; get high and fly away.
But, I realized that day, that it's hard to escape the things we can actually
see.
That, it's only when we come upon our snakes, that we are truly tested.
So, sorry Grace. Sorry, Snake. But we do our best when we're afraid and
if we're lucky we rise unscathed.
Blessed as the soil thirsted rain, with bodies made of blooded veins that
turn like serpents.
Claim your nature twisted Cain.
It's ok to be afraid. It's ok to be brave—sexy, wild, and enraged—you are
blood of holy made.
So, let your old skin break. Shed scales of loose weight and turn wild
twisted fate into a life that you can taste.
Each lesson born mistake, when we finally face our hidden snakes.

PUMA PERL

Death Valley Bodega

I don't know if my friend David Smith
died as he wished,
a white dove shooting from his mouth

This morning I woke wondering how close
the end is and which books
I will have a chance to read

My only hope
is that the dog goes first
She's not even mine and

I'm not anybody's
My kids deserve the relief
of unburdening my weight

if I ever grow as heavy
as my mother, or my father,
confused, peeing in the doorway

In Bodega Alley, the vet sits
in his wheelchair, surrounded
by clothing and umbrellas

His friend folds up the tent
Invisible city
down here at the bottom

Manhattan hides behind
cranes and jackhammers
We buy bodega coffee and dollar bagels

Diva waits by the fence, an unoccupied

blue beach chair left by her side
Nobody touches another's property in Bodega Alley

People know what is theirs
An open umbrella in sunlight,
a radio playing Harold Melvin

Wake up everybody
Hurricanes to the south of us
Construction northeast and west
Down here at the bottom
It looks the same
The children of nobody sleep in the alley

The men play dominoes on the corner
Wheelchairs cruise down the block
Diva waits for her buttered bagel

At home, I hear from a friend
She says she's dying
We all are, I think

Unsure of how to leave
before the party ends
While I still remember how to walk

BEGONYA PLAZA

Love

Love is the one feeling rising above all else thereof. Not a power tool to be used by the cruel fool upon weaker, ridiculed, and unschooled. Love is strength, God, courage. Hard to know love unless you show your woes, foes, and what you intend to sough. In love don't play the hero who purrs because your favors just might not be her's. A part of love is sex, that intercourse that can disturb and perplex, amongst uninterested strangers rushing to circumflex an itch, an ache, a burning rush without even a tender crush, just the desire for a violent thrush. A chew, a suck and to let out the gush. While this act can lead to more, the escapist and addicted think they can buy love at the candy store, like a craving tended to for which they implore. Yet found in the thoughtful whore whose carefree heart has capacity to adore, unshackled, unbound forevermore unrestrained, not making love a chore for which she was disdained. The sore decadent hardcore with no ration for compassion, unwilling to restore empathy instead of war, luring density yet lacking fidelity chasing after necessity, void of clemency looking for a freebie. Blindly misplacing the key to cross the soul's boundary, body holding on, suspicious and afraid the heart being swayed, betrayed or preyed upon like a delayed blockade. After reluctantly having paid and obeyed, the favor never feels conveyed except for being played.

The victimized fears being underpaid, launches on a crusade of lust and disgust, driven by mistrust in the banal hushed, unloved canal of agitated recreation where the ultimate revelation is degradation or speculation and final resignation, returning to love starvation, unaware that love is shared and not an obligation leading to accusation as if you didn't have fun otherwise why didn't you run before the devastation? Love begins within. Hold up your chin, protecting the skin, otherwise taken on a tailspin that makes you a mannequin. Heart pain is different in that you feel you've gained even when defamed and slain for truth has no shame nor anyone to blame. The dance was a generous act of free expression smacked with a balancing of torment and suspense the final recompense as spiritual consequence. Loving and being loved is the joy where two hearts ploy not to destroy the paper toy linking delicately together through stormy or sunny weather, free like a feather traveling clear wind, skin to skin innocent of sin, hearing the sounds of a violin playing Chopin's "Fantasie Impromptu" in a motor inn, or in East Berlin, no matter, the adventure's about to undo what you thought you already knew, and learn love goes beyond a casual screw as the alchemical mix of time and space with nothing to fix gives love its final brew. Eyes alive without disguise, fluent sighs intermingled with ancient outcries between ardent allies without compromise, or the need to fantasize, vulnerable, powerless, unprivatized or advertised, ageless, deathless, an awareness of its reflective presence. Transformative and gracious in the moment of parting and saying, adieu, the symphony was real, the bond stronger than steel, love was expressed through and through. Neither one was dormant but engaged and connected in the rendezvous forever imprinted in memory like a tattoo, though tough, still, just enough.

VINCENT QUATROCHE

The Missing Beat Link

In my mind's eye, I can see him sitting in a midtown bar near Penn Station over near 34th Street around suppertime in mid-October of 1961.

He's young and fresh off the train from Philadelphia in town to audition for a role in an off-off-Broadway play. He's nearly broke and nursing a stepped on flat draft and thinking he needs to find a job somewhere. Pronto. The jukebox is playing *I found my thrill on Blueberry Hill* by Fats Domino. By nature, he's minding his own business despite some random glances from a blonde down the end of the bar, "Good luck with that," he considers. "I'm broke and not Elvis."

So then in strolls this tall, dark-haired man, shy and strikingly good looking. He looks like a college half-back with quiet good manners. He sits down on the rickety stool next to our man, orders politely a speed rack whiskey.

They exchange wary glances. Big man lights a butt, produces a small spiral notebook, and starts writing in it. Phil sighs in relief. Well, at least he's not another a-hole with an ax to grind.

Lost in his own thoughts now, Phil barely sees the two other fellows enter the bar and surround his seatmate. Their intense animated enthusiastic conversation becomes infectious. Clearly, they know something that nobody else in the bar has a clue about. One is an intense-looking, thin Jewish guy with curly black hair and thick horn-rim glasses fronting wild eyes. His sidekick is a strapping, classic Roman-profile bruiser with a big booming laugh. Despite himself, Phil finds that he is eavesdropping until at some point when his glass has been dry way too long, the guy the other two call Jack, looks over at him with a big smile and asks, *"Hey buddy - want a drink?"*

RIVKE LELA REID

Tenth St. at Hudson (300 Words Out a Window)
November 2015 – Revised 2018

"I mean he just turned shrill!"
said one to the other walking out
of the door by my left shoulder

a fairly small Starbucks, but
one with available seats
as I wait for my first audition

Taxis are so square not - not unhip -
fuck Uber and the other hipster
union busters - no, it's just

they're crossover es-yu-vees now.
Well – there go a couple of sedans
to prove me wrong. Me, wrong?

I'm not wrong that was a pretty blond
with a green and blue scarf tied to her
bag strap – (hey, that's *my* trick!) to feel

beautiful – so another three second one sided love affair
ends. Anyway, the gal in jeans and glasses who didn't say
"isn't it too orange" after dying her hair

seems more my type. My type? What is
that, what can that be if I still am
working on my type? Looking out

the window – wanting pen, not laptop.
Looking out and charmed there's reproduction
going on some people clearly have real hope for

the future. I miss my non-existent grandchild
but I don't know what they would have to live through.
There's a reason we die. I guess I'm not ready to finish this role -

besides I have an audition in two hours.

JANET RESTINO

E. Coli Blues

(A cappella intro…a blues version of the Popeye song)
I'm weak to the finish
cause I ate my spinach
I got dem E. coli blues….
threw up on my shoes…. not because of booze... not seasick on a cruise

(Blues music comes in….in the key of G)
I got me a salad…with Feta cheese
some walnuts & dressing
hat spinach/ brought me/ to my knees

I got dem, I got dem, I got dem E. coli blues
that bag of spinach/was almost my finish
that bag of greens/that was the means
to dem E. coli blues…got dem E. coli blues…E. coli blues

I bought it at the grocery store
I tell you I ain't shoppin' there no more
I bought it in the produce section
damn sure I'll vote in the next election
'cause that FDA still is collectin' their pay
no more o' this shit – I bit & I got hit!
with **dem E. coli blues…E. coli blues…E. coli blues**

I couldda died!
been on my last ride/said goodbye to my hide
checked out on the world wide/had my insides fried/been washed out with
the tide

I couldda been dead!
lights out in my head/no more sex in bed
might as well have eaten lead/because of what I was fed

it was that spinach…it was almost my finish
E. coli blues…E. coli blues…E. coli blues

'Til the Doc came & fixed me
he got me an IV/it cost me a big fee
no more spinach for me…no more spinach for me…no more spinach for me
how 'bout some string beans? Maybe asparagus is safe…
O dem Brussel Sprouts/I got my doubts…think I'll grow my own…
E. coli blues…E. coli blues… I got dem E. coli blues…threw up on my sho-e-o-e-sss

STAN RIFKEN

Secular Thoughts and Prayers

If there is a God, that is master and creator of everything in the universe, how could he possibly let himself be represented by the clowns who claim to be his followers? What would Jesus think of the people who call themselves "Christians?" Would he even recognize them as Christians? One should call them "Christoids," not actually Christians but a remarkable simulation.

If you were to observe Christoid public behavior you might imagine that they practice a religion based on defending fetuses and suppressing gay people. That's the only time you hear about them.

They no longer feed the hungry, protect the weak, heal the sick, love their enemies, turn their other cheek, or any of the things Christianity used to be about.

If Christ hadn't risen, as they say, he'd be spinning in his grave, over the nasty, stuff being done in his name. These Christoid's existence should be evidence that there is no God. Because of there was a God, he would have already smitten these people for ruining his brand name.

What Christoids have done to the brand name "Christian," is what the Coca Cola execs did to "Coke" when they attempted to market "New Coke." Christoids will kill a doctor, for performing an abortion. A fetus is not-person, is more sacred to them then a doctor, who is a person.

They think they have an exemption on the "Thou shall not kill" commandment. They love the unborn, but they seem to hate the previously born. They show God's love by torturing homosexuals. They say God told them not to sell wedding cakes to gay people. What makes a wedding cake "gay?" Is rainbow frosting an insult to their lord? Why would a Christoid baker refuse to sell someone a cake?

The only difference between a gay and a straight wedding cake are the plastic figurines on top. A straight wedding cake has only a little plastic bride and groom on top. Never two grooms or two brides.

Perhaps a Christoid baker can just leave the plastic figurines off? Or give the customer a little bag, with two plastic grooms and two plastic brides. Then, it's the customer's choice to decide which ones will go on top of the cake.

Christoids want their kids to have a religious exemption from anti-bullying laws in school. They want their children to be permitted to beat up gay kids in their class. Their practice of faith is beating people.

They don't realize that religious exemption from the law could lead followers of another religion, to demand their religious right to sacrifice a virgin, as per instructions of their invisible friend.

I remember when we were told that Monotheism was a more advanced form or religious belief than polytheism. As if somehow, having one imaginary friend was better than having a bunch of imaginary friends.

Why is it less sophisticated to say "My god lives in the river," or "My god is the sun," than "My god sits in a golden throne in a cloud-filled place."

A real Jehovah would be embarrassed at the collection of nasty loons worshiping him. All the other gods make fun of Jehovah when they get together. Zeus, Thor, Ba'al and all the forest and river gods would shout across the celestial lunchroom, "Yo, Jehovah, have any of your followers blown up an abortion clinic or mosque, lately in the name of your LOVE."

The other gods mock Jehovah, calling him Mr. Mono-in-Monotheism. "Hey Jehovah, tell Jesus to seek medical attention if his resurrection lasts longer than four hours!"

If there really is a God of the Universe, on judgement day, I can just point out to him that no one could possibly believe he existed, based on the caliber of his most vocal supporters. If he really is as great as they say, he'll give me a pass, on having doubted his existence.

I have learned that all religions have one common message which could be summed up as: "DO WHAT MY INVISIBLE FRIEND SAYS, OR I'LL KILL YOU!"

JOE ROARTY

Poems of No Recompense

th co-operatv unity of mankind
glimpsd
n its amputatd pieces
its melancholy
& bad habits
th thoronss of th disastr
that it ntnds
that it has brot about
strewn
behind it
mor than burning bldgs
& th cries of th dispossessd
its outrageous lies
reducing truth 2 tears
that it kiks down th stairs
out nto th street
poems
of no recompns
mn w no fortune
th bittr life we lead
@ th bottm of th cup
nfamus
n th forevering nstnts
of its legnd
its vile reputation
its damnd salvation

STEPHANIE ROGERS

My Dog Doesn't Do AccuWeather

She looks up at me, brown eyes shining
and barks at me through a mouthful of leash.
I lean onto my side without getting up
to push her back toward her own bed
hoping she'll get the message.
Instead she licks my hand free
of the last crumbs of cheese crackers
I shouldn't have had the night before.

I scratch her between her ears
and under her chin
before rolling over to groan
at the gray sky
that snarls through my bedroom windows,
already damp with large, forbidding drops
fresh from the clouds
that are about to break.

It's Saturday; I know a storm is coming,
and I want the covers under my chin
securing the knowledge
that I don't have to get up early.
All she knows is that it's daytime again
and she wants me all to herself.

She barks at me again, more loudly this time
as the leash has dropped from her mouth.
Still she refuses to let her presence be denied;
she jumps up on my bed turns in a circle,
plops down in a heap of grey shag at my feet
and pouts for whatever she thinks she's missing outside.

JEFF ROSE

Flavor

I want a reaction from my general practitioner. He is a little guy that always keeps the same little smile but never laughs. I feel kin to these people don't react to anything. I don't really react to anything. There's something in that. Maybe I'm just trying to get a reaction in general. When I meet someone unflappable, I want to see them, well, flap. Perhaps that's how this all starts.

We're discussing my blood. It doesn't seem to have any vitamin D in it even after the supplements and extra dairy and eggs and sunlight, if you'll believe sunlight exists enough in February. My doctor says we may have to get an MRI or even go full colonoscopy.

"That's fine," I say. "You never get enough chances to see pictures of your own bowels."

No facial reaction. Just absolutely none. "Be careful what you wish for," he mutters.

Before calling down to the gastroenterologist and telling her to free up the lube and camera for another exploration, he says there's one more preventive test we could try, though it's new and a little controversial. He says that I can eat some of myself.

"I'm sorry, what?"

"You eat a little of yourself," he says. "We take a swab and send it to a lab upstate. They grow a bigger sample of tissue and send it back in a month. Then you eat it and tell me what it tastes like."

My doctor explained that the idea came from dogs that can smell cancer on people. Apparently, some dogs have the ability to sniff a person and detect by scent whether they have cancer and whether it has gone into remission.

Obviously, I don't know anything about medicine, yet this seems to make even less sense to me than usual. "How would I know what cancer tastes like?"

"That's why it works. You don't recognize anything. You should taste 'familiar.' Do you know the flavor of your tongue? You've spent your whole life tasting yourself without realizing it. So, the sample should taste like nothing to you. If you taste 'familiar,' you are healthy. If you don't agree with yourself, that's usually a sign of disease."

I imagine a little nugget of me about the length between two knuckles on a small plate like a boneless chicken wing. Maybe a side of blue cheese. My doctor dressed like a laconic sous chef. Thinking about it makes me want to gag. But I suppose I bite my nails. I can do this.

"All right. Prepare me."

So the nurse scrapes a little of me from my cheek and off it goes to be prepared.

****

The words of my uncle Dan come back to me: "Eventually we will all die eating ourselves!" Dan was the weird uncle. Maybe he really was a prophet. He holed himself up on the Michigan peninsula in a little cabin without internet, a phone line, electricity … a lot of guns though, my parents said. Never heard about what happened to him. Maybe I can find him and tell him he was right. Maybe he ate himself.

In four weeks, the sample is ready. Everything about the doctor's visit is the same. I wait for two hours past my appointment time in the waiting room. The nurse takes my blood pressure as if I'm not about to cannibalize myself for science.

My doctor arrives with the main course in a petri dish. It's a raw piece of me, sliced thin and long. Jeff carpaccio. Not sure why I imagined a little nugget. Not sure why I thought I would be cooked. I didn't expect a wine pairing or anything, yet the plastic fork seems a little unceremonious. I delay.

"You ever sneak, uh, a little bite of some of your patients just to see what they taste like?"

He ignores me. "Do you want to be alone while you eat the sample?" the doctor says.

"No, no. I got this." I pick it up with my fingers and drop it in my mouth like a sardine.

I'm not sure how many times I'm supposed to chew it – five, ten, thirty times? It's too late to ask, I don't want to talk with my mouth full of myself.

Here's all I learn: I'm not a delicacy. Mushy. Tasteless. Less than tasteless actually. I taste like air. It's hard to recognize the flavor from any other part of my mouth. He's right. I'm essentially swallowing my tongue. I suppose I once thought that I'd grow monstrous with time. Something malignant feared, and powerful. Instead, as I chew, I find myself to be a soft nothing, so easily scraped off, copied, and digested.

We still don't know why I don't have any Vitamin D in the bloodstream. But at least we know I don't taste like a deficiency. And how many times do you get the opportunity to find that out?

MARIE A. SABATINO

What the Hell is Love?

I am seven years old and I know one thing for sure: I love those beautiful brown rabbits that my daddy brings home for me, and my brother, and my sister. We take care of them nice, feed them real good, and they become bigger and bigger every day. We name them Bugs and Elmer.

What I don't know yet is that their necks will be snapped and there will be a sharp, popping sound confirming their demise. Easter dinner. "Che bello," daddy says.

At twelve years old I think I love the corner of the bed, as my best friend, Dawn, teaches me what happens when we open our legs, and climb on top, pushing ourselves against it, over and over again, riding the perfect edge like a pony, giddy with joy at this new discovery in her bedroom attic.

At thirteen years old I want to love French kissing—really I do—but it's like drinking a giant fishbowl of saliva with a snake jumping out to attack you.

At fourteen years old, I have my second French kiss with this bad-ass, black kid who's two years older than me, and therefore far more experienced, and I learn that I love, love, love French kissing after all.

At fifteen, I wait desperately for love.

At seventeen, I meet Ralph and as much as I try to catch up with love, I never do, and so now love waits desperately for me.

I have no idea what to do with this love that begs and pants like a hungry puppy, so I make out with Ralph's best friend. But Ralph forgives me so I have to do the dirty deed of breaking up with him instead. Fucking good guys, I think to myself. Stay the hell away from them.

At twenty I fall unabashedly in love with an artist and he falls even worse for me. He teaches me everything I know about love and he teaches me about the giving of oneself with your soul.

So of course, I destroy this love by the time I am twenty-one.

At twenty-one and a half, I think I might love someone else, a writer who plays guitar, and looks like Ethan Hawke when he was in that *Reality Bites* film.

The Ethan-Hawke-Look-Alike doesn't love me back. But he is absolutely in love with my mouth on his penis. Then the mouth gets terribly bored or is it the penis that gets bored first? I don't remember. And so the penis and the mouth go their separate ways.

At twenty-four I move to the East Village and fall in love with another artist. I try cocaine for the first time, then I try it again, and then, I try it some more. We drink lots of vodka at KGB Bar, we write poetry with black magic markers on my bedroom walls, and we make suicide plans in the early morning hours before we fall asleep in one another's arms.

But we never see it through. The suicide. Or the relationship.

In the remaining years before I turn thirty, I collect men on the Lower East Side the way my mom collects pretty-smelling candles. The candles last much longer, of course.

At thirty, I fall in love again, once more with a writer. He is nineteen years older than me. And he treats me like a mouthful of strawberry-flavored, Bubblicious bubble-gum. I am a giant bubble of euphoria. Life could not possibly be better than this.

At thirty one, I fall in love with a fetus that I cannot touch or hold or rock back-and-forth but there it is, the doctor says pointing at the screen, there it is growing inside of me, and before I know it, there it is, the heart that suddenly stops beating, and then there it goes dying, someplace deep inside I can't even see.

I cry the cry of the hysterical every time I sit on the toilet for the next several days.

When it is all finished and done with, I cry even more. Then I cry some more and more and….

Later that year, I fall in love with a mutt. They say maybe she's a Jack Russell maybe a Beagle maybe a Pit Bull mix. She is the worst animal in the world. She despises every single dog in all of New York City and she wants to massacre each and every one of them at all times. Going for walks with her is like going to war.

It turns out that I love that little devil-beast of a mutt more than I love any human. Except for maybe my kid nephew. All right, I'll call that a tie.

A few years later, the little devil-beast of a mutt gets cancer and she's not even five. I'm in ten thousand dollars' worth of debt from all the doctor's visits and the surgery and the chemotherapy. She dies anyway.

And it's like my heart finally throws in the towel.

Everything falls apart in my relationship of seven years.

I tell him it's over and that I'm leaving.

He doesn't stop me.

I move out two weeks later.

I promise to never fall in love again. Never ever never.

I begin to write these stories about my life. And I think, maybe I even love them a little, too.

But I can end them whenever I want, put them away when I am finished.

This past summer, I meet someone new. He's not an artist. He's not a writer. Maybe what one would even call an ordinary guy? Of course, he's slightly out of his fucking mind, too.

Once again, he's nineteen years older than me. He's had plenty of joy. And plenty of heartache, too. When I'm not with him, I feel dizzy and lost. When I am with him, I feel safe and sound.

Is that what love is? Those simple moments when time is on pause, and your heart is at ease, and there is a body holding the entire length of you, making you feel without a single care in the world, everything safe and sound.

So, I think to myself: Maybe I'm finally ready to stop running from love.

But…. Just don't hold me to it.

LINDEL SANDLIN

Shadow Boxing

Long-denied resentments,
after years of being tamped down,
come screaming into the daylight
like a great, black-winged banshee.
Hideous and unwanted emotional dross
sears my psyche.
How could I - sweet, caring, spiritually evolving little me --
feel such seething animosity for someone I love?

Well, how dare she trigger ancient wounds
by not caring for me
the way I needed my father to show me love!
Wait… what??
Who said that? That's fa-KAKta!

Wow! Now that this Shadow Story
has geysered up,
how shall I dispense with it?

Can I steadfastly subdue it
as if it were some hideous bridge troll?
Hoping that when faced down,
it will allow me to pass --
even offer up its treasure to me?

Perhaps I must engage in mortal combat
with this, my own murky specter
blasting it into a thousand tiny shards.
No, that won't do!
For what if those tiny resentment shards
all take root and grow into a dark forest of angry reeds?

Fantastic! Now, I'm in a 1950s sci-fi movie!

Mind is constantly running amok.
By turns, frightening itself
and then amusing itself.
Denying itself
then over-indulging.
Here I am in this place of Wit's End
having forgotten what propelled me here in the first place.
Oh, that's right -- the Screaming Banshee of Unreleased Resentments.

Maybe I'll just give that ole banshee a hug and
offer it some chocolate.

CHRISTINE SANTELLI

For You

And summer months it stays and stays
A blind man's gaze through the haze
Of glory days that he would not waste for you
Cigarettes and old blue jeans
A drink of wine in child's time
A sidewalk crack with growing grass
An open-door hearing children laugh for you
A carnival a party clown
To spend a day without a sound
A foreign land a shooting star
A firefly lighting up a jar for you
An open field and open sky
A lightning storm soaring way up high
A canopy to shade the sun
A nice cold beer when day is done for you

ERICA SCHREINER

Farm Dream

you're awake and I'm awake
and if we had a farm it wouldn't be unusual for us to get up now
every morning we would rise and beat the sun
bare feet on worn hardwood
you put on your coveralls
and I live in sundresses
and we let the weather age our skin
in the traditional sense
I collect eggs
and you take out the dogs
and gather hay
you feed the cows
I milk the cows
and head back to the house
but first I
set down this heavy metal carafe
and pick some wildflowers
snap the stems with my calloused hands
pink and purple and golden like hymns
and daisies
I push open the screen door
drop the flowers in a mason jar
start breakfast
fry eggs and bacon on the cast-iron
fresh milk with cream on top, still warm
we don't bother to refrigerate
I look down at my feet
and realize they're kind of muddy
I forgot shoes again
instead
we are two insomniacs
alone in two apartments
sending messages back-and-forth through glowing screens

MICHAEL SCHWARTZ

Dumplings and Beer

No, this is a late-night comedy sketch. It has to be. This can't be happening. How can this be happening? How could she have already made the call when they just said it was too close to call?

As I watched his victory speech with my mouth hanging wide open like my older brother's did when he was fast asleep in the back of my father's car on long trips in the summer and my other older brother and I holding in our laughing put orange slices on his tongue until he bit down and woke up in confusion with juice dripping down his chin and Watergate pouring out of the car radio, forty-three years later sitting in the living room alone I slowly put one steamed Chinese vegetable dumpling after another into my own mouth, each one seasoned by the saltwater of my dripping tears washed down with a bottle of Fat Tire New Amber Ale. I'd been ailing for a few days with a bad cold and had to stay home from work. By the night of the election, it had gotten worse, but I wouldn't go to bed until the results came in. Now they were in and I wondered how I could sleep.

It was 3:30 in the morning and I prepared for bed to try to escape the nightmare. I looked at myself in the medicine cabinet mirror thinking that maybe *I* was the reflection and that the face looking back at me was the real me, and would tell me that actually, on the other side of the glass she had not yet conceded and they were doing a recount. It said nothing, other than that the real me was under an evil spell and had been turned into a spotted gray frog with padded double bags under its heavy-lidded red eyes, an amphibian physiognomy no self-respecting fairy tale princess would ever lower her standards to kiss, no matter how much I tried to convince her I was once a prince, and that if she was faithful to the bedtime story and did what it says she's supposed to do to transform me back, we would live happily ever after.

Just in case she changed her mind, I wound the waxed floss around my index fingers, pressed them firmly with my opposable thumbs, those unsolicited reminders that I was still a member of the pathetic human race, and began to stick my hands into my wide-open mouth to get to those hard to reach cracks between my back teeth, when suddenly all the televised toxins I'd ingested for the last eight hours began to gurgle and boil and rise up inside me. I closed my mouth and held it all in.

Oh no, uh uh, I am not going to throw up; the only imminent thing around here is sleep, and I'm right on my way to my room. When I said during his speech that I think I'm gonna throw up I meant it metaphorically, not literally!

Then, as I deliberated over the decision of whether or not, in spite of my fear of food fungus festering on my gums all night long as I slept, I should forgo flossing for the first time in fifteen years, I exploded like Mr. Creosote the gargantuan gourmand after gorging on a multi-course meal in Monty Python's *The Meaning of Life*, vomiting violently and voluminously loud for a very long time as I stood over the bathroom sink. I thought about falling to the floor and holding my stomach to make it less painful and easier to push it all out and doing it in its proper place, the toilet, but I had to maintain *some* sense of dignity, and the thought of sticking my head in that stinking bowl reactivated my gag reflex, so I never had a chance to make it to my knees anyway. Every time I thought it was finally over, there was this one piece of stubborn carrot that stayed stuck in my throat, causing the whole process to start all over again. And I hadn't even *eaten* any carrots! I thought I was going to choke to death. I knew my retching wails had woken up my cat Bella, who had wanted so badly to stay up for the election results but just couldn't stick it out, and that now she was probably scared and wondering why an elephant was giving birth in the bathroom. That was the sound of the rigged system, I would explain to her later.

I guess shredded cabbage and bok choy packed into a pillow of sticky white dough washed down with fermented barley, hops, and piss water don't mix well with a lacerating cough, globs of green and yellow brown shnot backing up into my brain, and a genetically modified cornhusk haired jack o lantern faced mob infested empty casino carny huckster ballyhoo shpieling lost little boy trust fund baby crying under his nasty narcissist bully headed hunger for his Steeplechase Park smashing to build a white's only apartment complex father's love pathologically lying conniving trophy wiving sire of trophy hunting power suit wearing leopard killing cowards erecting luxury towers homelessness causing tax break to billionaire giving bankruptcy declaring disability mocking water boarding border wall building innocent teenager lynching lacking introspection fiddling with his hubris on his golden penthouse throne speaking in superlative self-aggrandizing generalities to cover up an ignorant incoherent set of policies boasting pussy groping because when you're rich and famous you can get away with never finishing a sentence to get out of answering questions so many accusations of sexual molestations anti-intellectual last book read was way back in high school hate speech spewing journalist suing free speech screwing pointing finger fidgeting on the hair breath trigger of the nuclear code neo Nazi endorsed racist misogynist homophobic xenophobic birther movement leading temper tantrum Tweeting NRAnal violence inciting ad hominem attacking parents of Muslim American dead soldier insulting terrorist inflaming climate change denying health care obliterating tax evading hypocrite under indictment J Edgar Comey-intelpro November surprising aspiring real estate agent defrauding worker and contractor stiffing outsourcing jobs to third world country child sweatshop laborers with tiny hands like his to stitch his school assembly presidential debate red satin neckties environment destroying animal torturing undocumented kill floor slaughterer and assembly line butcher crippling factory farm T bone steak hawking spouting oil rig sucking ancient sand dune destroying Scottish home bulldozing family displacing for golf course constructing coal mine promising alternative energy green job revolution poo-pooing fracking-bring-backing Supreme Court stacking to make America great again by becoming ordained to officiate the wedding vow renewal ceremony of Uncle Sam and Ante Bellum slavery preserving electoral college closed down polling sites in neighborhoods of non-whites nonvoter blaming but refusing to take responsibility for their own inability to galvanize the electorate like the one who should have been the Democratic nominee would have done Democratic National Committee and ratings craving corporate media created creature of society's celebrity worshipping numbing comfort. I should have gone to bed at ten.

YUYUTSU RD SHARMA

Latina Love

Latina love found me
in a bustling NYC party accidentally

Latina love took me
to be a shaman, for sure

my black bag bulging
from magical rainbows,

serpents from a Hindu Heaven,
skull of an abducted female Yeti,

magic mushrooms,
Yarchagumba and other Himalayan aphrodisiacs

to raise even
a stodgy stone from its Amazon sleep.

Latina love adored
my pagan adulation of her long brown legs,

golden-limbed goddess
inside her spacious body's wide sanctuary

Latina love wished to
make love to me all night long,

translating my works
except love poems into Spanish.

Latina love wanted
to rent my brown body, turn it

into a sacred sutra,
a Sufi song or a shatoosh shawl

to wrap around her shoulders
all the time in all NYU parties

Latina love said
she understood sanguine silence of my snow peaks

Latina love
wanted some action right away,

flowers of wild passions wet
from her impassioned breaths

"Can you read my future," she asked,
spreading her palms after the waves had receded,

"Maybe there's a Juju
in the spidery maze of these heavenly alleys."

Latina love
wanted to be a wife I already had.

VERANDAH-MAUREEN SHEPARD

Without Ceasing

If I'd known the last time, I hugged you
and this moment
would be separated by eternity,
I'd have hugged you without ceasing.
I'd have memorized
the worry lines
in your forehead whenever something thought provoking crosses your
path–
…for the record
there are 4 and a half
and the top line extends the longest.
I'd have
memory foamed
the tone
of your voice
first thing in the morning
when you roll over and belt out good morning baby in that sing song
guttural growl.
I'd have taken care to study how
your embrace in daylight
differs
from your embrace in nightlight
from behind like
all you've ever wanted,
and some of what you didn't think to ask for
was safely nestled between your heart and your forearm.
If I'd have known that eternity could be
4 minutes
38 hours
and 7 weeks,
I'd have dreaded this moment.
Spared myself

memories
of what used to be
and loved you without ceasing.

EDMUND SIEJKA

The Waitress

The night before
A heavy rain had fallen
Traffic lights,
Hitting the streets
At just the right angle,
Transformed wet asphalt
Into endless black ribbons
Stretching,
Straining,
To touch the horizon.

Opening the heavy double doors
To the Diner
He saw that most of the tables were taken
But there was one left
All the way in the back.

She was there
Calling all the morning customers by name
The men answering good naturedly
Their voices still heavy with sleep.
 He watched as she walked
Down the narrow aisle
Every so often resting on a familiar shoulder
As she leaned over to pour another cup of coffee.

Closing his eyes
He wished she was with him
Kissing him
Her arms around his waist.
He, holding her so close to him.

When he looked up

He was alone.
Eventually she came to him
Walking all the way to the back of the Diner
A mischievous smile on her face
Her arched eyes
Impatiently asking
"Are you ready to order now?"

MELANIE SIROF

Copa

She is the only girl in class
With a flower in her hair
And though it is not yellow
Nor feathered, I see Lola
In her prime before Rico
I see the smoke
And Lola's cha-cha
Which is altogether different
In the hips from the
Dance she does for Tony
On the empty dance floor

This girl is not Lola
She is nine and rapt
Watching her teacher's
Colored pencil merengue
Across the paper
The music is in
Her head and
Her fingertips
Waiting her turn
Always waiting her turn

The flower
Black and crystalled
Removed earlier that morning
From the dog's misbehaving mouth
Tells me she knows
Her turn is coming
And unlike the boy
With his finger
In his nose, she
Will be high-heeled
And ready for it

CHLOÉ SKYE

Pleasure

But is this generation's view of sex and love really so grim? [...] Our data has shown that one of the greatest contributors to hookup behavior is a desire for sexual pleasure. -from CNN's "Young adults and a hookup culture," by Ian Kerner, published May 16, 2013

This summer, I have lost track
Of how many times I've had to cancel plans and say
Sorry, I have to go home
Immediately, but leave out the
To masturbate and write poetry
Part.

I've lost track
Of the virtual pages written speculating
On youth culture. Read: irresponsibility.
To hook up - as ambiguous as a tangle of wires
Each of whose kisses
Spark electricity as they connect.

Words take up all the gaps yet leave open
Tiny spaces for fear
To turn to sudden, fervent honesty
Which burns too fast for regret.
That what you condemn is actually what you want.
That someone's unwitting kindness has healed you
More fully than your capacity to express gratitude.

His greed between my legs is the biggest turn-on.
I butterfly for him; he pushes apart my wings.
My pulse: the drumbeat of *want want want.*
Our bodies the two curved petals of a tulip
Arching towards each other; in the space between them.

- pleasure, satisfy. The words have an old-fashioned grease
And they slide from the gap I mean to fill.
To do what you want.

That pleasure feels good.
Then you hook up the wires and electrify yourself.
The microscope has turned inward but we're not learning anything new.

The problem with being full of words is they can be misunderstood;
The desire to continuously repeat, "You're amazing"
Is not understood like a kiss.
Yet this is the only way to say
I'm glad my body is of use to you.

MOIRA T. SMITH

The Beginning of Magic

The beginning of magic is knowing what you want,
knowing yourself and what is appropriate for you at a given time.
The beginning of magic is knowing what you want,
while aligning yourself with that which is appropriate.
The beginning of magic is knowing yourself, acknowledging all there is of
you.
The primal beast. The tender heart. The chaos of confusion. The
crystalline mind.
The impulse of evil. The soul of compassion. The thought-seed of sex.
The hunger of desire.
The beginning of magic is a torch casting its glow into the spidery corners
of your mind.
Reach in-- and examine the festering wound. Greet the child that waits
there,
silently guarding the gift of pure sight. The terrifying gift.
Grasp the hand-- thrust out from the abyss. It's your own.
Now untie the knot at the heart of your denial. Pick at the knot at the heart
of your denial.
Tear at the knot at the heart of your denial. And if all else fails, do like
Alexander—
and chop it with the sword of your will. Unmask the lie-- the burdensome
lie.
Exchange the weapon of judgment for the tool of discernment.
Surrender to the alchemy of truth, and find rest there from the effort of
turning away.
Offer your innocence-- the root of your fear, knowing you may be ripped
to shreds.
Sacrifice your illusions at the altar of *what is*, and go begging at the gate
of the whirlwind.
Be kind. Spiteful. Wary. And open. Be silly. Dead serious. Holy. And
profane.

Take a good long look. Take a good long look, and recognize it all
as *you*.
Now look closer. The beginning of magic is in the mirror.
Strip naked and engage yourself unflinchingly there.
Lovingly and mercilessly interrogate your doubt. Day-- and night. Day--
and night.
Stalk your doubt-- day into night, until the stink of your wound, the taste
of your pain,
the discomfort of your first guarded encounter with joy
lead you to engage the flitting shadows of your being. Then choose where
you stand,
and ally yourself with those aspects that reflect your true nature.
Learn to control those that might undermine your stance,
and remain open to altering your position in light of new information.
Then you will begin to be conscious. You will begin to embody the power
that is available
for use in the pursuit of wholeness, that in time your integrity may serve as
a touchstone,
a lighting of the way on the pilgrim's path of doing-- and *un*doing.
Loose the knot at the heart of your denial, and cultivate your magic-- for
the sake of all.
It is our primary duty, and one that cannot be shirked.
You must become your own spell, elemental and enduring. There is no
spell without you.
Your hand-- putting a match to the flame. The flame-- putting a light to
your mind.
Your mind-- putting your will to the task. The task at hand: *you*. There is
no spell without you.
So lie down on your belly. Lie down on your belly on the ground.
Lie down on your belly beneath the moon, and clutch the earth,
the rich moist body of all that's come before us, the pulverized bones of
ancient friends,
the crown of the mulching dead who sustain us. Inhale their pungent
remains.
Give thanks, and then pray to the mother. Pray face to face with the
mother.

Sink to her breast-- her dark fertile breast, and whisper your tale of woe.
Chant, chant-- the absurd precious story of your pain. Cry to the mother--
for all you've lost,
and all you've never known. Lie down on your belly and weep to the
mother.
Weep. And that will be the beginning of magic.

COREE SPENCER

A Broken Heart on E7th Street

In the late 1980s, people who live in Tompkins Square Park shanties or the surrounding area in the East Village are fed regularly by The Bowery Mission, Trinity Parish on Ninth Street, or the Hari Krishnas.

Our managers at 7A Cafe allow me to feed homeless people day-old bread and leftover home fries during my daytime waitressing shift. 7A Cafe is across the street from Tompkins Square Park so we're right in the midst of the homeless population and park squatters.

When I hand out leftover French bread and potatoes, a few of the homeless men offer responses such as "Does the bread come with a free beer? Cause the Hari Krishnas always give us something ta drink like Kool-Aid." There's the man who, when offered bread, like a great Shakespearian actor, dramatically grabs his stomach and says, "I cannot digest bread, only meat: medium rare, with an ounce of liquor."

I have one regular homeless customer, an old man who spends his days pacing up and down Seventh Street between Avenue A and First Avenue, never going beyond this block. He walks, appearing to contemplate life with his hands clasped behind his back like a monk, sometimes stopping to peer up at a building, shading his eyes. He's grizzled, covered in several layers of clothes, with the last layer being a huge, gray, army trench coat like the kind Sargent Shultz wore in the TV show, Hogan's Heroes. The coat is belted off with a rolled-up trash bag tied around his waist. He wears a wool cap and army-issue boots with many plastic shopping bags stuffed into them.

"What's your name?" I ask the man one day. He replies in a foreign language, or is it gibberish? He walks away from me, then goes up to a nearby parking sign and shakes a finger at it, continuing to speak in this unknown language. He wanders a bit further, swinging his arms wildly until he ends up at the corner of Seventh Street and Avenue A where he turns around. Then he mutters to a sad, leafless little tree as if it's his friend.

The only time he seems to become lucid and speaks a few words of English is to make sure I get his food order right. In fact, he doesn't care if I'm in the middle of taking a paying customer's order. He'll tap me on the shoulder if I'm in the outside cafe and when I turn around, he says, "Now, miss. Food. I eat!" I hold up a finger and mouth the words, 'okay, one minute'. He nods 'yes' vigorously, and walks away. But a moment later I feel that familiar tap-tap on my shoulder. I try to ignore him until my customer tells me my homeless friend is back. I turn and he says again, "Miss! Now! Eat!" If I'm inside the restaurant taking an order he'll rap on the window, and when I look up, he'll point at his mouth — signaling he's ready to be fed. He just won't leave me alone until I fix his bag of food.

Since he won't tell me, through trial and error I've figured out his precise order: five pieces of French bread, five pats of butter, and three grape jelly packets. Two napkins join all this in a plastic to-go bag. The first few times I just dump a handful of bread, butter, and jelly into a paper bag. He opens it, counts everything, then either hands me back extra items, or holds up an item and says, "More, more!" Once I get it right, I give it to him. But he hands the bag right back to me.

"No, it's for you, not for me." I say, holding it out to him. He says something I don't understand while pointing repeatedly down towards his feet. "You want the bread and butter in your boots?" I snap at him, then glance over at the customers in my section holding up their empty coffee cups for a refill. I sigh and wave the paper bag at him again.

"No! No! No!" he says as he pushes the bag back in my direction. Then he bends over and pulls on the many plastic bags poking out of his boots. I have no time to do pantomime with a homeless man while paying customers who will leave me a fifty-cent tip need my attention.

I slap my forehead. "You want it all in a plastic bag!" It turns out he has a certain distaste for paper bags.

He also refuses a plastic knife as if it's an indignity and an insult to offer him a fake utensil. He wants a real stainless-steel knife. I actually never see him eat the food I give him, making me think he must go further down Seventh Street to eat where I can't see him. Despite living out on the street he seems to be a very private person.

He always returns the knife saying, "Clean. Miss. Clean!" I thank him. It looks spotless, but despite this, I still toss it into the bus pan so Flaco, our Mexican dishwasher, can give it a once over with soap and hot water.

At work, he becomes known as "Coree's homeless man", as if I've adopted him. When I'm not at 7A, the other waiters tell me he spends his days peering into the windows of the restaurant looking for me. Two waiters, Philip and Susan, try feeding him, tossing any old food into a paper bag, even after I've told them exactly what his order is. He won't touch it. He paces back-and-forth, stopping only to mutter, "Miss? Where Miss?"

It feels like he's some poor alley cat I've started to feed and now depends entirely on me to survive. After I move from Brooklyn to the East Village on Eleventh Street, only four blocks away from 7A, I try to stop by on my days off and feed him. Otherwise, he drives everyone crazy. If I can't make it, I'm greeted at my next shift by my manager Marina saying, "Your boyfriend was looking for you all yesterday. Look, Coree, you still can see the grease spot on the window where he pressed his face up against the glass." He's one of about half a dozen of my "boyfriends", sad guys, some homeless, some able to afford the $1.85 breakfast special who visit me regularly at 7A. I'm popular with the guys no one else wants to wait on.

He never answers any of my questions. What's his name? Does he have a family? Does he ever want some leftover home fries? This leaves me to wonder where he sleeps at night. He's never around past eight or nine o'clock when I work the late-night shift. I do know where he pees. He pulls a giant plastic cup out of one of his many plastic shopping bags he keeps parked in very specific spots on the sidewalk as if it's his outdoor studio apartment. His hand burrows into the multi-layers of clothes and the first time when I realize what he's up to, I quickly turn away. Once he's finished, he tosses the liquid into the gutter, shakes the cup dry and slips it back deep into his shopping bag.

One slow, sunny day I'm working the outside tables at 7A when I spot an old Polish waiter smoking by the front door of Leshkos Diner across Seventh Street. I run over.

"Hey, do you know anything about that guy? Like his name?" I ask, pointing to the old man, who's near the back door of 7A, his hands behind his back, peering into our old green dumpster.

"Oh. Him. I do not know his name. He old Polish man."

"Why does he just walk up and down this block all the time?"

"I hear long time ago he fall in love with Polish girl. Very beautiful girl, who live on this block. Ask her to marry him."

"Wow! Really?" I look over and see the old man is now staring down Seventh Street, shading his eyes. Then he starts to amble off with his hands clasped behind his back towards First Avenue to finish his stroll. "Yes," the Polish waiter says as he watches the man and takes a drag from his cigarette. "I hear she no return love for him. So, he vow he never leave this block. Until she say yes, and marry him. Now, he never go past this block."

"Where's the girl?" I ask.

"Oh, I never know what happen to her. She maybe move away? Or die. Or she maybe still up there?" He says as he nods toward some apartment windows on a building in the middle of the block.

"Which apartment?" I ask.

"Oh, I do not know." He sighs, shaking his head, as he finishes his smoke. He laughs a little and says, "She maybe still want to think about if she want to marry him? Who know?"

The next day I ask the old man about this supposed love interest. He shakes his head adamantly, waves me off, and walks away muttering in what I'm guessing is Polish, without even taking his plastic bag of food.

I tell the other waiters at 7A what the Leshkos waiter told me. They think it'd be a great idea to fix the old man up with one of the bag ladies in the neighborhood so he won't be so lonely. They suggest maybe he might like the lady with the filthy old makeup and smeared lipstick who pushes a cart filled with dirty newspapers, or how about the freckle-faced lady who laughs hysterically for no reason? They tease me about making up two plastic to-go bags of French bread for them to enjoy a picnic lunch together next to the green dumpster outside 7A.

They just don't get it so I tell them, "A man who's sacrificed his entire life for a specific woman wouldn't settle for just any old homeless lady."

When I quit working at 7A and then move to East Fourth Street I see less and less of the old man. One day I see him and he looks thinner, despite his many layers of clothes. I go into 7A and ask the waiters if they're still feeding him. They say that they try, but he keeps asking for me, peering into the windows and watching everyone who comes in-and-out the door. They let me fix him a plastic bag with his five pieces of French bread, five pats of butter and three grape jelly packets. I even convince them to let me give him a real knife. "He'll give it back. I promise."

When the old man sees me, holding out his plastic bag he scuttles over. He grabs it this time, yelling at me in Polish. He turns and storms off.

I guess like the girl he loved many years ago I'm just another woman who's let him down.

A few more years pass and I stop seeing him altogether. No one I ask seems to know what happened to him. The waiter at Leshkos shrugs his shoulders, "Who know? Maybe finally he leave the block? Or find new girl?"

Or, I think, did he die? I wonder if that's true, is he now reunited with that Polish girl of his dreams? Or sadly, is he forever pacing back-and-forth on the East Seventh Street section of the Great Beyond, still waiting for her answer? I hope wherever he is, someone is getting his French bread, butter and jelly order right. And making sure to put it in a plastic bag with a real knife.

PETER SRAGHER

The Ancient Mariner
Bucharest, Romania - January 2012
to Phillip Giambri

i will join you
       over seas
       and oceans
to find the real mariner
         the ancient mariner
         the valiant mariner
the mariner that loves fishing
       for words
and turns them into
       a boat
 and sails with his
       thoughts
from coast to coast

       no stop
       no stop
       he cannot stop
cause he's the breath
       of the wave
cause he's the storm
       of the sea
cause he's the shark
       haunting the weak

the ancient mariner is always
       on the move
meandering over the
       salty waters
his wishes and hope
and he will drink
       the waves

and sinks his sails into
      the coral reef
to find a colour
      a colour for his soul

ZEV TORRES

Hold Off

Hold the questions until
Attendance has been taken
Credentials have been checked
It is confirmed that everyone has paid their tuition
Yesterday's assignments have been collected
And everyone has had an opportunity
To review the updated syllabus
Until the presentation is concluded
The applause has died down
And the students have had a few moments
To catch their breath and
Share their impressions with one another
Giving our venerable speakers time
To slip out the side exit
Before being pressured to account
For their dubious methods.

JOHN J. TRAUSE

We Have Always

Nail a book onto a tree
Memorize a word or three
Bury coins and golden watches,
Curios and witchy swatches.

Run around the yard and garden
Let your heart and feelings harden
Tidy up the little hollow
By the creek, both deep and shallow.

Put the sugar in the cupboard
Hide the watch behind the floorboard
Entertain the guests at tea
Memorize a word or three.

Store the books and don't return them
Someday you will have to burn them
Memorize a word or three
Someday you'll live merrily.

And remember, come September,
To be kind in May, November,
Even when the world's an ember
And you are its only member.

JOHN TRIGONIS

Dirt Cheap & Lovely

I remember when Daffy's used to be our date spot.

We'd spend an hour or two scavenging the sale racks
and discount shelves for half-off tags on
everything from charging iPhone cases and Indian
spice racks to unseasonable wears at
very seasonable markdowns.

At least once a month we exercised our rights as
*Supermarket Sweep*ers & bargain-basement vagabonds,
strip-searching all the faceless mannequins that
dare stand fashionably in our way.

Those aisles were mapped out in memory foam.
The mirrors forever reassuring us, *in writing*,
that we looked good.
And we never plotted the same course twice
along that Middle Earth of forever curving grid work
between launch & final clearance.

The day Daffy's closed its doors for the last time,
I bought myself a blue Italian-made trench coat for $25
right before I discovered you should
never trust a man in a blue trench coat,
never drive a car when you're dead.

(I never did trust that old self of mine, anyway.)

I can't remember what you bought that fateful night,
my dear, but whatever it was, I'm sure
it must have been dirt cheap.

And looked lovely on you, too.

ANOEK VAN PRAAG

Train

Stepped out of the freezer box into the sun
The weatherman told me so
but forgot to warn me about stormy winds
that knocks me down
The sun goes a long way
but when I miss the train
the world runs off
I fall off in a nightmare
try to catch it grab it
Jump on endangering myself

Then I let it go disappearing in the tunnel
sucked in by a sinking feeling
I should have seen the signs
the one minute sign
read the small letters at the bottom
what did I miss?
The boat?
wait for the next train to come?
if it does…. it may never….
the discomfort of not knowing
learning to not know
if there will be another one
for me

ANGELO VERGA

Los Angeles

The childish ravings of the famous
Pass for wisdom, also no adversary
Can wound more than bad advice.

This is a century of murder,
I am a war poet, the moon
Wanes, and the ebb tide roars.

They say if you tip the planet on its side
Everything that's comes loose
Will wind up in Los Angeles.

I'm so grossed out right now,
I could puke, or I could talk.
But would it help?

It doesn't work if you don't want it to.
This is not right, he said to his whiskers.
Consider the source, boys and girls.

MARGARETTE WAHL

Lunar Pilgrimage with Shazia

"Hussain is from me, and I from Hussain." Prophet Muhammad

Walking for two to three days, 80 kilometers.
This religious pilgrimage
from Najaf to Karbala.
Shazia with thousands
walk in freedom.
Bystanders make bread in barrels
hand-out water, kiss the feet of walkers.
Symbolic for a time, weapons were placed down
allowing the *walk of the free.*
Men, women, families celebrate
a prophet.
Not frightened, this once war-torn place
we witness the unity of people, safe in Iraq.
Her videos show a shrine,
the size of a concert arena.
Peace walks in sand.
Next year's walk depends
on the phases of the moon.

GEORGE WALLACE

Unemotional

it was the old reggae it was the one-stop flimflam it was a
very good ride a big move a big mistake and she with those
flimflam tears and she with those flimflam eyes and she lit
me up and okay she smoked me right then and there and
she was not even a fast one was she honey no! she burned
real slow and she burned bright steady and right through me
like the green surface of the sea slipping slo-mo through the
guts of the globe

     'o crocodile' she smiled 'i love you so'

and she bit me and i bit her back but i didn't bite long or hard
enough and here's the long and short of it 'no no she said you
do not know' she said 'no no you are not the one' it was a gris
gris get-even hoodlum voodoo moment the same old same for
me and i don't know how high in the sky a man has got to go to
be the unemotional one -- but up i go, every time,
i go up every mountain and i run and i run til the mountain runs out
and when i reach the top i touch the sky and say
'how many how many lord how many times a man got to'
and i say 'lord tell a man'
    and the lord says 'i know son I I know '
and the lord he says 'and by the way
    you know i know, you know'

lord know it

i say this over a thousand times
it's a kind of a prayer

ROBERT WATLINGTON

Radical Love Making
(Miss-cegenation)

On a hot sunny day
I see a beautiful Black sister
And wonder what has made my
Affections sway the other way

I think of my beautiful mother
And the support she supplied my pop
Tho' surrounded by what could be called poverty
She continually strived for her family to be on top

Sixties, drugs and hippies
Scattered by loyalties to my race
Here I thought my limited education
Would make me a White in black–face
O, how I humped Asia, Europe and Africa
Never looking above their waist
As time went by
The hair grew less curly that
Stuck between my teeth
My beautiful wonderful Black sisters
Grew impatient—dating blond boys with names like
Hans, Werner and Keith.

I still grow uneasy when
I see you hugging eyes of blue
Yet I still think I can savor Gerta
As well as stick it to you
I look at my Rainbow-colored offspring
Wondering what their futures will bring
I will never desert their mother
Tho my moods and feelings swing

Strange how these relationships
Rarely end in marriage
The cat runs off
An' all that jazz
No sirree, I'm not gonna be
One of those brothers
I've got too much pizzazz

EYTAN STERN WEBER

Heritage

I found my heritage in a postcard. Dated like any other piece of post, August 23rd, in ordinary, old-world script. Stumbled upon during the standard closet cleaning at my grandmother's apartment. I first held the browned, brittle paper like a sheet of so thin glass.

I began to read the claustrophobic scribbles when I realized that this analog item, this opaque screen needed no projected pixels to come alive as a four-dimensional window into a place and a person. This scrap of dying memory was the vertex at the intersection of time, chance, and humanity that manifested itself as my great grandfather.

This postcard wasn't just, "Wish you were". This withering wisp of once-white scroll was, "I love you, and I need you, so much so that I won't even tell you this is the last you'll ever hear from me."

Because this postcard was sent from Paris in 1943, a few days after Passover seder. I know this because every Passover, I see...I used to see the youth, the fear, the tears in my grandmother's eyes as she recounted the tale of black uniforms storming in mid-seder that one damned year, and how the last time she saw her father, her vision was obscured by crimson and white armbands.

As the last vestige of communication, we can know my great grandfather ever sent, sitting in a filth-ridden, overcrowded Drancy soccer stadium, he wrote, "Tomorrow, I'm being taken to an unknown destination with a thousand others." And in that moment, his hand reached through the ink and took mine, so as to brace me for what was to come. "Mes chères, si je souffre, c'est seulement pour vous parce que je sais pas dans quel état vous êtes. Je vous embrasse en vous priant d'être calme." My dearest ones, if I suffer it is only for you, for I don't know that you're okay. In my mind, I'm holding you in hopes that you'll stay calm." He lied to them, and told them all would be well. He talked about clothes, friends, finances. He loved them too deeply to collapse in fear from what everybody knew: the cattle cars left full and came back empty. A few more weeks, if not days of denial was the only gift that could be given by a man stripped of everything, by sacrificing the chance to say goodbye.

He receded back into the lines of lost stoics and the paper seemed to crumble. In oh so little matter and mentality, I met a man and I felt his fear, I learned of life and love, and felt a resilient sense of pride that I could call that Giving Tree a part of me. I found my heritage in a postcard, and I haven't looked at pen and paper the same way since.

SUSAN WEIMAN

Roommate #6

"So, do you want me to be your roommate or not?" Bess asked.

We were on the N train returning from Barnes & Noble where I was meeting Bess for a second time. It was the end of the month and I was desperate.

"Yes," I said. That was my first mistake.

Bess was in journalism school and now worked as a reporter for a local newspaper. Three months after moving in, she quit her job. She complained bitterly about being unemployed, and increasingly became more depressed.

"'I'll never get a job. They only hire graduates from Columbia," Bess whined.

"If you get out of your pajamas and left the apartment, maybe you'd have a better chance of finding a job." That was my second mistake.

Then she met Mark. They spent most evenings across the street at a Lugo's drinking and making out at the bar. Most of the barflies ignored them except those looking for a fight.

Halfway into the month, she informed me she was moving out to live with Mark and asked for her security deposit.

"No way," I said. We had an agreement to give notice on the first of the month. You can't walk out now." Bess retreated into her room.

The following evening, I arrived home to find Mark photographing each room in the apartment. "Hey, this is private property. Put down the camera."

Mark yelled at me and told me I was no longer allowed to speak to Bess.

"She's my roommate, and I want to speak with her directly -- not through you."

"She's no longer speaking with you. Besides, you better return her security deposit. If not, I'll make your life miserable. I'll ruin your credit and ruin you financially."

"Get out!! Get the fuck out of here!" I screamed and phoned my friend Jonathan who lived two blocks away.

"Be there in a minute. I'll beat the shit out of the guy."

"That's okay Jonathan. I can handle him. If it gets worse, I'll call."

I stepped into the hallway, and in a calm authoritative voice, l asked Mark to leave.

"Give her the money!" He shouted as he hovered over me and pinned me against my bedroom door.

"You better get the fuck out or I'll call the police."

A few days later, I received a summons from housing court. The bloodhound reporter and her sidekick were after me. I had charged her an additional $40 a month in a rent-stabilized apartment.

With no other recourse, I made an appointment to see a landlord-tenant lawyer, who advised to pay back the additional rent. Also, I learned that a verbal agreement would not hold up in court.

Now I was out the security deposit, and a couple of hundred dollars, not to mention, in two weeks, I had to find another roommate.

FRANCINE WITTE

Send

Yes, my text-only lover, I have a life,
and it's not about you. It's not about you
and me holding hands IRL. It's not about
the clammy vinyl of cars seats on hushed
summer nights. There was a time when romance
was an open mouth waiting to taste the moon.
But like one breath making room for the next
breath, things have to move on. The cascade
of emoji hearts is no longer enough. But don't
worry, I will store it in the archives, and when
I die and detectives search my phone for clues,
they will find you. Then, they can relax their
clenchy shoulders, nod at one another and agree
that yes, it appears that I was loved.

MICKEY WYTE

The Kid from Brooklyn

I slipped into Mulroney's around 3 p.m. The place stunk like a week-old bar towel. My eyes squinted, adjusting to the darkness. Two rummies near the front end of the long mahogany bar sat shrouded in a cancer cloud as thick as the air over a Jersey oil refinery.

At the center of the bar sat a construction worker on a liquid break. He was two hundred and fifty pounds of muscle if he was an ounce.

I walked to the far end of the place and parked my ass on a stool.

The bartender, let's call him Jake, 'cause that's what he looked like he should be called, stood hunched over the bar, *The Racing Form* spread between his bent elbows.

Jake grunted, "Whadaya have?"

"Rheingold," I said.

The kid strolled through the door a minute after the train screeched to a stop on the El above Mulroney's. He was told to look for the man in the hundred-dollar suit and black fedora—me!

"Find your way from Cropsey Street ok?" I asked.

"Yeah."

The kid's hair was thick, black, and greased back into a Duck's Ass. He wore a white Tee, khakis with a studded garrison belt, and hard leather shoes.

"They say you got good hands."

He strutted over to the center of the bar.

"Hey, Mack."

The two-hundred-and-fifty-pounder looked up from his liquid lunch.

That's when the kid fed him a knuckle sandwich, sending the bum tumbling off the stool onto his keister.

"They don't call you Johnny Thunder for nothin'," I said.

"I get the job?"

I stood up, threw a crisp twenty down on the bar, and flicked the brim of my fedora with my finger.

Jake grunted and turned a page of the *Racing Form*.

Stepping over the poor bum out cold on the sawdust floor, we left Mulroney's. Me and this tough kid from Brooklyn had some serious business to take care of uptown.

ANTON YAKOVLEV

Cold War Accessories

The seafront promenade is longer than childhood
and spirals through all manner of fourth walls.
We glide into the Baltic Sea to reach
St. John the Divine. Classic dolls mill around
its makeshift yard, interviewing each other.

Some have learned twelve-tone laughter.
Those who do penance mostly stay out of view.
Where did all the owls get to?
Their eyes used to comfort me.

I will not rest until every letter you write
resembles a bearded statue projecting a false security
on what is essentially a castrated symphony.
It always comes down to the death of stars, doesn't it?
I will hammer my wooden clogs on your podium yet.

SUSAN YUNG

Work in Progress

Before IRAQ war
B4 WTC
B4 Homelessness
B4b4 Unemployment

B4 Tiananmen Square Massacre
B4 the Sandinista & Noriega War
B4 the Marcos Dictatorship by being Ronald Reagan's puppet
B4 the Confucius Plaza Demonstrations for Worker's Rights
B4 Civil Rights Movement
B4 Hiroshima Bomb
B4 the Freedom of Slavery ... the civil war

We are now there.

NICK ZAHARAKOS

Holy Mackerel

I go fishing for the Halibut
But I get the Blues
If, by some Fluke, I Flounder
and only catch a Crab

To any of you;
Guppies, Snails, Stingrays,
Shrimps, Sharks or Jellyfish
out there
Who don't dig my Whale of an epic

This old Seahorse,
As endless as the foamy waves,
With hook, line and sinker proudly proclaims:

"Frankly, my dear
I don't give a Clam!"

For Pop,
Your loving son

ALANA ZONAN

Time

Feels like six tons
of air inside.
Cramped teeth
with words to hide,

Hydrochloride eyes
reflects the mind's
pithy pride.

All emotions aside.
Letters like "I"
phrases like "I don't know"
catch my attention
in a repetitive lingo.

How much is in my control?
Or, better yet, what even is?

Days I can't remember.
Cab rides with absent members.
Tongue flaps,
self-slaps,
fucked-up crap,
in every pen tap.

Fact: Life is unfair.
So, why live it
if you're frail?
Bound to fail.

When all seems stale
could you follow the trail

of all your insecurities?

The clock is ticking
But not on my watch
We stand here frozen
In the space that time forgot.

Afterthoughts on Pre-gentrification

SUSAN YUNG

Suburbanizing LES

In 1972, I had been a cultural worker for Basement Workshop, a non–profit community cultural arts center in Chinatown, with 50 other Asian Americans. Contrary, I became an activist by initiating the Confucius Plaza demonstrations in 1974 so that garment and restaurant workers can ascertain better jobs in the construction businesses. We succeeded with 40 Asian workers in construction. Later, I helped renovate an 8,000 sq. ft raw loft space into an arts institution, presently Museum of Chinese in America (MoCA). At that time, we had workshops in writing, dance, theater, darkroom, and archival materials. Now MoCA only exhibits old stuff. I even curated the first Asian American exhibit in NYC; performed at Charas on 9th St.; read poetries @ Nuyorican Poets Café with Lois Elaine Griffith; participated and documented A Gathering of the Tribes until their big move from E. 3rd St. to E. 6th St.; worked with Rome Neal's "Banana Puddin' Jazz" at Nuyorican Poets Café and read at Bowery Poetry Club; curated a women's art exhibit at Bullet Space; group show at 123 Rivington Gallery where I met Bobby Watlington, a Black artist where we read at 3 of Cups' Ancient Mariner's open mic.

On the day of my induction as a Silver Tongue Devil, there also was an important event for "Basement Workshop's 45th Year Reunion" held in Tribeca's fancy restaurant by Asian American Arts Alliance. I had to be there to promote Asians in mainstream arts. First, I showed up in Tribeca to introduce my guest, Ed Primus, nephew of Pearl Primus, (African anthropologist and taught Alvin Ailey African movements), to the Asian cultural community. Ed's daughter had learned Chinese where a conflict had erupted with a "corrupt principal". He needed judicial support and began mingling among the Asians as well as take photos. I left and quickly grabbed a taxi during rush hour. It was the slowest "red–light" ride to LES. I showed up in my fancy frilly dress wearing a Tibetan necklace and read for 15 mins. my Trump Story. I quickly returned to Tribeca with another slow taxi ride. There, I realized, Ed had a problem getting seated among the Asian men. He was about to leave. After musical chair maneuvers, Ed finally got to sit next to a dynamic lawyer. Whew, I was able to relax with Asian entertainments, good wine & steak dinner.

These past five years, I have been associated with non–Asians, and Blacks. I spent most of my life "blending" in a diverse LES community; explaining its diverse foods; the subcultures of squatter living; the problems of closing small businesses & non–profit arts organizations. This when, the stratified ostracisms between Whites and Minorities, in an overdeveloped community, has broadened.

Once upon a time, the war on poverty was expressed with murals depicting social changes for working-class families. (see Marlis Momber's "Viva Loisaida" video) Now, this duality of being "American Born and Foreign" * is a perpetual competitive battle to become a mainstream artist.

"BIG FUCKIN' MIKE" LOGAN
EAST VILLAGE STORIES

THE EMPRESS JOSEPHINE,
QUEEN OF THE UNION SQUARE KRUSTY KIDZ,
CAMPED OUT IN THE NO LOITERING ZONE
OF ZECKENDORF TOWERS,
SAFELY COCOONED WITHIN A RAT'S NEST
OF RUBBISH AND REFUSE...
HER LOYAL
BRINDLE PITBULL... " HERBIE "... IN TOW... A
HAND LETTERED, BLACK MAGIC MARKER
" PLEASE HELP "CARDBOARD PANHANDLER'S
PLACARD PROPPED ON THE GUM LITTERED
SIDEWALK IN FRONT OF HER... STARES
BLANKLY, UP AT ME... IN A DRUG - INDUCED
STUPOR...THROUGH INNOCENT, DELFT CHINA
BLUE EYES...

IN MY FANTASY... SHE ESCORTS ME TO THE
HOT SHEET HERALD SQUARE HOTEL... WE
RENT A ROOM BY THE HOUR... WE SHOWER
TOGETHER FOR HOURS... SCOURING YEARS
OF GRIME AND DIRT FROM HER PALE, WHITE,
TRANSLUCENT SKIN, UNTIL HER HIDE GLOWS
PINK FROM SCRUBBING... LATHER UP HER
TANGLED WILD RED PUBIC HAIR PATCH...
UNTIL HER CROTCH IS AS FRAGRANT AS A
GARDEN OF CHAMPAGNE ROSES...

... LEAP AS A COUPLE, ONTO THE FRESHEST
LINEN SHE HAS EVER EXPERIENCED, IN HER
ENTIRE ADULT LIFE... EAT HER PUSSY UNTIL
HER PUDENDA BUCKS UP AGAINST MY FACE
LIKE AN ANGRY JENNY MULE... WE FUCK FOR
HOURS... UNTIL WE COLLAPSE INTO POST -

COITAL COMA...

WE SLEEP... ENCIRCLED IN EACH OTHER'S
EMBRACE... LIKE TWO NEWLY FOUND
SPOONING LOVERS FOR WHAT FEELS LIKE...?
DAYS... UNTIL I GROGGILY AWAKEN...ALONE...
ONLY TO DISCOVER SHE HAS STOLEN MY
WALLET, WATCH, GALAXY ANDROID PHONE,
ALONG WITH MY SHOES AND PANTS... AS IF

SHE WERE SOME CHEAP, STREET - WALKING,
HOOKER, ROBBING HER DRUNK, PASSED OUT,
OUTTA TOWNER JOHN... IN SOME LOW RENT
SLEAZY MOTEL ROOM ON THE LAS VEGAS
STRIP... WHICH...? SEEMS PRETTY MUCH
WHAT HAS JUST...? HAPPENED TO ME...

... SO MUCH FOR THE FANTASY....

WHAT WOULD YOU EXPECT FROM EMPRESS
JOSEPHINE, THE QUEEN OF THE UNION
SQUARE KRUSTY KIDZ... ANY WAYS...?

STEVE DALACHINSKY

NYC 9/18 - the times have always been changin'

Be it music, poetry, art, booze, the places that have come and gone in the lower east side are staggering, particularly since the '80s onward and more so in the past five years. I will not chart their courses by naming all of them individually but suffice it to say those that remain which sustain some semblance of cultural or actual drunkenness have become fewer and fewer. I can however state that art galleries seem to flourish at an astounding rate and many of these host poetry events. One such is White Box. And there are bars like Bowery Electric who have back rooms or downstairs areas for what is mostly rock-related culture and at least one poetry-oriented event. For poetry, there are maybe in the downtown area five venues on the lower eastside that have it fairly often some of which are very particular in the gigs they present. There are also three or four on the west side, (Many having been driven further out into Brooklyn or uptown or Queens). Those remaining on the east side include Parkside Lounge, Sidewalk Café, KGB Bar, The Poetry Project at St. Marks Church (some fifty years running at this point), the part-time Bowery Poetry Club, the stalwart Nuyorican Poet's Café, and of course pop-up events here and there like at 5C Cultural Center or various art galleries throughout the lower Manhattan area. But with the absence of Fusion Arts Museum, Tribes Gallery and many bars a toll has definitely been taken on the poetry world.

As for the lower west side, there's Cornelia Street Café, the Zinc Bar, and further south, Poet's House (again a venue that is very particular with their choice of readings/lectures).

What am I getting at here? Simple. Our lower Manhattan choices have been drastically cut down. Especially in the vital East Village/Lower East Side scene. So, what can we do? What we must do in their stead is to do what Philip Giambri has so ardently fought for with a hand-full of others: keep the scene open and vital at all costs by presenting/organizing as many events as possible in just as many venues.

So, let's raise our glasses and make a toast to the sustaining health of the arts in the Lower East Side and elsewhere.

C. O. MOED

Last Call

We all heard the news. Developers had just bought East 14th Street and were going to raze everything, including the Blarney Cove.

I had passed the Cove for years. Never went in. I went to a dive on St. Marks until an unfortunate incident. (Hint: don't have a bad affair with the bartender of a bar you call home unless you don't want to hang out there anymore.)

Besides, the Cove didn't seem like a place for a girl like me. Those guys were having shots at 8 in the morning and I was too old for that kind of pissing contest.
I was also too broke for more than one round. Not when for an extra $5 I could buy the bottle at Astor Warehouse.

So, I'd pass the Cove and never go in. Even after the neighborhood blogger, Goggle told me it was great. Even after I married a new drinking partner.

But suddenly it was now or never. I said to the husband, let's go to 14th Street. We need socks and a couple of places sell a dozen for $6.99. And then maybe after, the Cove for a drink.

We headed east but the further we got the worse things looked. It was like Close Encounters of the Third Kind when Richard Dreyfuss slipped into the restricted area and saw all those dead cows.

Store after store were empty with 'For Rent' or 'Going Out Of Business' signs in the windows. Even the cheap department store was gutted - 40 years of affordable shit, gone.
There was only one cheap stall left in the last remaining tenement. The guy there told us the landlord had refused to sell to the developers, but eventually, they'd win and buy the place – "They always do", he said. Meanwhile, he had a dozen socks for $5.00.

A couple of steps east was the Cove. We peeked in and saw Christmas lights twinkling and a baseball game on both TVs.

"If it's the Yankees, I'm not going in...." the husband mumbled.

They changed one of the TVs to the Mets vs the Marlins, we got Rolling Rocks in big-ass glasses because Pabst only came in tall boys, and the guy at the end of the bar played every baseball song on the jukebox for us, including one about being a Mets fan (which really should be categorized as a mental disorder).

I asked the bartender when they were closing. "End of June." she said. "It's sad."
Then a couple of more regulars came in. The bartender spoke to everyone, everyone spoke to everyone and I said to the husband, "Well, if we were not old hermetic writers who were always broke, this would be a good bar for us."

The 6th inning made it clear the Mets would lose. Again. The beers were $3 each.
"Leave a big tip," I told the husband.
"$2?"
" $3."
After all, they were closing and we weren't going to get another chance before the end of June to say goodbye to a bar that, if we weren't too old, too broke, too hermetic, we'd go to.

Silver Tongued Devils

March 2013-March 2018

Bookings and Biographies

Bar 82

Thursday
March 7, 2013
Verless Doran
Mariposa Maria Teresa
Fernández
Duane Ferguson
Pauline Findlay

April 4, 2013
CANCELLED
No Venue

Identity Bar

Thursday
May 2, 2013
Saroya Marsh
Peggy Friedman
Michael Lydon
Mariel Pauline

June 6, 2013
Gordon A. Gilbert Jr.
Aimee Herman
Kofi Fosu Forson
Qurrat Ann Kadwani

July 11, 2013
George Wallace
Maya Osbourne
Jaime Martin
Moira T. Smith

August 1, 2013
Joyce Hanson
Mickey Wyte
Ann Herendeen
Danny Matos

September 5, 2013
Brother Mike Cohen
Susie DeFord
Jean Lehrman
Thomas Pryor

October 3, 2013
Peter Story
Jherelle Benn
Johnny Cashback
Donna Bailey

November 7, 2013
CANCELLED
No Venue

December 5, 2013
CANCELLED
No Venue

Three of Cups Lounge

Wednesday,
January 22, 2014
Janet Restino
Mitch Cohen
Nicole Acosta
Tru Lyfe

February 27, 2014
Robert Gibbons
Stephanie Rogers
Russ Green
Ronnie Norpel

March 26, 2014
Simone Davis
Harry Rolnick
Karen Levy
Dominique Fishback

April 30, 2014
Barbara Aliprantis
Wayne Kral
Michelle Seabreeze
Angelo Verga

May 28, 2014
Veranda-Maureen Shepherd
Graham Willner
Multiya Vision

June 25, 2014
Alessandra Francesca
Daniel Guzman
Marie A. Sabatino
Vincent Quatroche

July 30, 2014
Simone Nikkole Azúcar
Richard Fein
Lorraine LoFrese Conlin

August 27, 2014
Jane LeCroy
Bernard Block
Meliora Dockery
Thomas Henry

September 24, 2014
LinDel Sandlin
Matthew Abuelo
Ast Maat

October 29, 2014
Luis Cordova
Donna Bailey
Nick Zaharakos
Saara Dutton

November 19, 2014
Angela DiCamillo
Joe Roarty
Nicole Ferraro
Peter Storey

December 17, 2014
Eric Alter
Marie Chisolm
Leslie Goshko
Ptr Koslowski

January 28, 2015
Richard Allen
Diane Block
Zev Torres
Jenna Lynch

February 25, 2015
Margarette Wahl
Ed Siejka
Eve Blackwater
Yuyutsu RD Sharma

March 25, 2015
Amy Barone
Michael Schwartz
Veronica Gollos
George Wallace

April 29, 2015
Michelle Carlo
Creighton Blinn
Vicki Iorio
Joel Louis Gold

May 27, 2015
Jeff Rose
Viviana Grell
Michael Anton
Holly Hepp-Galvain

June 24, 2015
Mike Logan
Anoek van Praag
Ron Kolm
Robin Bady

July 29, 2015
Steve Dalachinsky
Boni Joi
Vincent Quatroche
Jennifer Harmon Gersbeck

August 26, 2015
Nichole Acosta
L. R. Laverde Hansen
Rachel Therres
Peter Blaxill

September 30, 2015
Roya Marsh
Ann Herendeen
Charly Fasano

Anthony Moscini

October 28, 2015
Howard Finger
Maria Lisella
Gil Fagiani

November 18, 2015
Brian Sheffield
Patricia Carragon
Christina Fitzpatrick
Vogue Giambri

December 16, 2015
Gabriel Don
Art Gatti
Duane Ferguson
Jerry T. Johnson

January 27, 2016
Peter Marra
Virge Randall
Arthur Nersesian
Coree Spencer

February 24, 2016
Austin Alexis
Begonya Plaza
Burt Baroff
Linda Kleinbub

March 30, 2016
Craig Kite
Blair Hopkins
Kevin Becker
Jessica Adams

April 27, 2016
Francine Witte
Pauline Findlay
Ember Flame
Yi Wu

May 25, 2016
Susan Tierney
Scott Gawlicki

Michelle Carlo
Petey DeAbreu

June 29, 2016
Marie A. Sabatino
Vincent Quatroche
Jessica Adam
Anthony C. Murphy

July 27. 2016
Too Tall Jonz
Jasmine Farrell
Madeline Artenberg
Johnathan Cherlin

August 31, 2016
Valerie Keane
Matt Pasca
Terri Muuss
Sara Morgan

September 28,2016
Puma Perl
Denver Butson
Susan Yung
Marcus Bowers

October 26, 2016
Jason Gallagher
Kurt Nelson
Peloquin
Eytan Stern Weber
Alana Zonan

November 30, 2016
Bernard Block
Julia Ogilvie
Richard Newman
Anoek van Praag

Holiday Break

January 28, 2017
Joel Louis Gold
Anoek van Praag
Ron Kolm

Jane LeCroy

February 22, 2017
Brendaliz Guerrero
Olivia Greyson
C. O. Moed
Leah Gonzalez

March 29, 2017
Beth Corliss Lamont
Stan Baker
Janet Restino
Luciann Berrios

April 26, 2017
Creighton Blinn
Sandy Simona
Anthony C. Murphy
Ilsa Jule

May 24, 2017
John Trigonis
Susan Weiman
Erich Slimak
Emily Elizabeth Lazio

June 28, 2017
Vincent Quatroche
Barbara Ann Branca
Alec Miniero
Erica Schreiner

July 26, 2017
Liesl Clouse
Anton Yakovlev
Chloe' Skye
Safi Brown

August 30, 2017
Saara Dutton
Maggie Nuttal
Christine Santelli
Melanie Sirof

September 27, 2017
Jennifer Juneau
John S. Hall
Eve Brandstein
Jean Le Bec

October 25, 2017
Stan Rifken
Jasmine Farrell
Peter Marra

November 29, 2017
Deborah Clapp
Linda Lerner
John J. Trause

Holiday Break

January 31, 2018
Cancelled due to illness

February 28, 2018
Linda Kleinbub
Taylor Mali
Judith Lee Herbert

Last Rimes Show
March 28, 2018
Shannon McGarity
William Considine

Scheduled but canceled
April 25, 2018
Thad Rutkowski
M. C. Neurd
Rivka Lela Reid

May 30, 2018
Jim Hawkins
Pat Christiano

June 27, 2018
Christopher Grigsby
Robert Watlington

Matthew Abuelo is a writer, professional blogger, and award-winning poet. His books Last *American Roar* and *Organic Hotels* can be found on Lulu.com. His third book is *The News Factory* (Plain View Press). Matthew is a journalist for the online news site Examiner and recently worked for the Times Square Chronicles as a housing rights journalist and political commentator. He has performed throughout Manhattan including The Poetry Project's "Marathon," which featured, Pattie Smith Susan Vega, Lenny K, Steve Earle, and other icons. He is currently working on his fourth book of poetry, *City of Red Nightmares*, and a first novel.

Nichole Acosta is a queer, multicultural, diabetic, poet, born and raised in Brooklyn, New York. Her work focuses largely on human nature and the light and darkness that can be found in everyday life. "The Silver Tongued Devils are to me a family of storytelling barflies and adventurers. It's never a dull moment and I always learn something new."

Austin Alexis "The Rimes of the Ancient Mariner Reading Series stands out in my mind because of its cave-like atmosphere. That snug basement room. That dusky lighting. The take-home work from my teaching job keeps me from attending the readings at Three of Cups as much as I'd like. But I plan to show up more often this special year, as the series celebrates turning five. My only other definite literary preview for the near future is that I have work forthcoming in the upcoming Great Weather for Media anthology."

Barbara Aliprantis A Trilingual (English/Greek/ASL) Storyteller/Impresario, spotted Phillip Giambri, a few years back in the audience at the Cornelia Street Cafe. He had her from day one with the twinkle in his eye, winning sly smile and love of the spoken word, be it stories, poems or works of art. A mutual admiration society developed instantly! After participating in the "Rimes of The Ancient Mariner" series, Philip dubbed her a Silver Tongued Devil, presented her with a dazzling T-Shirt, which she proudly wears! In 1997 Barbara, founder of the "New York STORY Exchange" launched the longest continuous Storytelling Series/Open Mic in NYC at The Cornelia Street Café.

Richard Allen A Miami native, and fan of the spoken word, Richard Allen, divided his misspent youth between Los Angeles and New York before settling into NYC as a permanent home in 1988. He began writing in 2001 for the Fahrenheit Open Mic monthly readings and has kept the series going for seventeen years. Allen has traveled to Berlin, Lisbon and other cities for pop up shows and has been featured in documentary films such as *This is Berlin Not New York*, *Dolls of Lisbon* and *Self-Medicated*.

Michael Anton has been a professional photographer for forty years, the past ten as the official photographer for the NYC Department of Sanitation. **"I've** been thrilled to be a Silver Tongued Devil, and I love being an audience member as well. I've heard poetry and prose that have left me in a state of awe. I'm a sixty-year-old lifelong Manhattanite. My college years and a brief childhood stay with relatives during my parents' first divorce, being the only exceptions. My current artistic obsession is Albanian Cold War-era bunkers."

Madeline Artenberg "I'm proud to be a Silver Tongued Devil who featured at the exciting Rimes of the Ancient Mariner series, hosted by the cheer-leader for creativity, Phillip Giambri. Being taped on that stage has been an important experience. Second or third time I performed on the open mic was memorable: Stressed from work, I grabbed the wrong page. Mortified, I asked if I could go off-stage and quickly grab the correct one. Many in the audience yelled out, "Let her do it, we want to hear her." Phillip created a family. Here's to moving it to another home."

Simone Nikkole Azúcar "Becoming a Silver Tongued Devil marked my emotional return to the mic. The love I received was genuine each time I graced the stage, especially when I debuted my graphic novel, *4A*. I could do anything and the crowd would travel with me. As a Brooklynite and Jamiricubish writer, this is why I love printed word; the concentration transports you to a different world. My upcoming projects include a poetry book, *Soul Under Water* and a film, *When I Thought You Left*. Purchase *My Journey though Poetry* and *Sidepiece Sanctifications* on Barnes&Noble or Amazon websites."

Stan Baker is an actor, comedian, playwright, lyricist. His credits include commissions/productions/appearances/readings at venues such as The Public Theater, New York Theatre Workshop, La Mama E.T.C., Dixon Place, P.S. 122, Theater for the New City, The Lark, HOME, The York, Cherry Lane Alternative, Columbia Univ., Cornelia St. Café, Village Gate, Bitter End, The Improv, Catch a Rising Star, Max's Kansas City, Danceteria, Folk City, and King Tut's Wah Wah Hut. Stan is often referred to as The Human Television. He loves the theatre as much as he loves to surf.

Burton Baroff "I have no glittering past, and as I begin my ninetieth year a modest glow will be joyfully embraced. Having read on open mic and as a Silver Tongued Devil, I count The Ancient Mariner shows rather than sheep for napping and at night. A few of my poems have been published which is nice, but not nearly as nice as the writing."

Amy Barone "I take my role as a Silver Tongued Devil seriously. When I get behind the mic at Rimes of the Ancient Mariner readings, I become more of a storyteller than a poet. Video-taping us gives every reading clout and adds a dose of seriousness. They aren't dress rehearsals. Like the Ancient Mariner, I'm from the Philadelphia area, so we're kindred souls. He gets me. He's an inspiration." Amy's poetry collection, *We Became Summer* (New York Quarterly Books) was recently released and her chapbooks include *Kamikaze Dance* (Finishing Line Press) and *Views from the Driveway* (Foothills Publishing).

Kevin Becker "Getting up in front of a NYC crowd is scary. Every time. But Mr. Giambri and Co. go out of their way to make me feel welcome and part of the family. I grew up above a tavern my mom and pop owned in Bayonne, New Jersey. I learned a lot about humanity and God's love for us in that place. It shaped who I am as a man and how I write as an artist. I've released a small body of my work and performed that work live at the Off-Broadway Triad Theatre NYC."

Luciann Berrios "My experience with being a Silver Tongued Devil was incredibly uplifting. When reading at Three of Cups, the warmth, support and feedback received from the audience and Phillip Giambri really inspired me to keep going, to keep talking about the truths I was passionate about, and to stay true to my own voice." Born and raised in Astoria, Queens, NY, she published her first manuscript *Thunder and Sunshine in One Body* (2017 Fly by Night Press). Luciann compiled and edited an anthology of her work and nine other poets, all-female/nonbinary, and artwork entitled *Women of Eve's Garden.*

Peter Blaxill is a retired theater professional, having worked on both sides of the footlights. **As** an actor, he has appeared on Broadway, Off-Broadway, Off-Off-Broadway, The Kennedy Center, extensively in Regional Theater and Summer Stock. He studied poetry with William Packard, Pearl London, Colette Inez, David Trinidad, and others. Peter's been a featured poet at The Cornelia Street Cafe, Su Polo's Saturn series, Mike Graves's Phoenix Series, and has been a long-time Open-Mic Gypsy at Rimes of The Ancient Mariner. His poetry has appeared in the Riverside Anthology, The Jefferson Market Anthology, and The New York Quarterly.

Creighton Blinn "In poetry, the difference between spoken and written word is an intriguing one. All writing has a distinct beat to it; even the most plainspoken prose has a specific rhythm which would be reflected in the author's reading. Yet poetry's structure is often more amorphous, the punctuation (let's be honest) somewhat haphazard. A looser framework allows for more ambiguities. Sometimes I'll discover that a set of verses which blend one way on paper, break in an entirely different manner when recited. A successful poem is one that does not force such conflicts into resolution."

Bernard Block "I first read at Identity Bar in July 2013. Packed! Phillip Giambri laughed at my poems. Returned in August. He laughed again. I "was in!" Featured twelve months later: August, 2014. Phillip laughed (perhaps shed one tear). I "was in again!" Prefer Spoken Word—poetry written to be understood." Bernard was born and raised in Bath Beach, Brooklyn. Cornell/Brooklyn College/Haight Ashbury/ Prospect Heights. Published: Levure Littéraire: Thirty-eight poems. Signature Series: Whitman to Ginsberg, Cornelia Street Café, six years. First full-length book of poems: *Am I my Brother's Keeper.*

Diane Block "My experience as a "Silver Tongued Devil" in the Rimes show has been an altogether positive one. The only negative in this equation is I don't get there as often as I'd like, primarily due to my violin teaching and performance commitments on Long

Island. No wonder the Rimes show is thriving. Phillip makes each spoken-word artist on that Three of Cups stage feel as though her voice deserves to be heard, that her work has merit." Diane is a native New Yorker born in Jamaica, Queens, raised on Long Island, and "awakened" in Manhattan.

Barbara Ann Branca After retiring from university life as a science teacher and author, she returned home to this creative community, just as she's always returned to her hometown, New York. "I'm especially glad my two grown children were able to hear stories of the environment, music, and family heritage that I shared with or sang to this receptive, supportive silver-eared audience that helped me find my poetic voice. I've been compiling what I've done on the stage as well as on the page. The former always seems more authentic, dynamic and fun! Thank you."

Eve Brandstein Born in Czechoslovakia, raised in the Bronx, poet, Eve Brandstein has been a major studio, network executive, producer, director, writer/creator, and casting director. She is also an artist, psychotherapist, and workshop facilitator. Her poetry appears in national publications, eight chapbooks and she is the author of the non-fiction book, *The Actor*. Eve produces Poetry In Motion, since 1988, a bi-coastal spoken word series bringing leading poets, actors, writers, and is a musician for eclectic spoken word events at Beyond Baroque in Los Angeles and venues in New York. She is a publisher of *The Hollywood Review* an anthology of L.A. poets.

Denver Butson has published four collections of poetry. His work has been featured in major anthologies and literary journals, on National Public Radio, and elsewhere. Butson has been thrice-nominated for the Pushcart Prize (once by Joyce Carol Oates). His collaborations with musicians and visual artists premiered at Court Tree Collective in the sum of uncountable things, a month-long book launch and exhibition in 2015. Butson is Co-Founder and Creative Director of BACAS, an international arts and cultural center, launching in southern Italy summer 2018. He lives in Brooklyn with his wife, actress/activist Rhonda Keyser, and their daughter.

Michele Carlo an author/performer who has appeared across the U.S. including the Moth's GrandSlam and MainStage shows in NYC, on NPR and the PBS TV show "*Stories from the Stage*". Her memoir "*Fish Out of Agua*" (Citadel 2010), about growing up in 1970s NYC, is also a podcast where Michele interviews artists of all disciplines about the work they do... and why they matter.

Patricia Carragon is a widely published writer who loves being a wild and sensitive Silver Tongued Devil. She'll never forget the time she performed *New Utrecht Avenue* and asked for audience participation. Originally a spoken word artist, Patricia also writes short stories, flash fiction, haiku, and more. Patricia is a Brooklyn resident who began her writing career in Astoria, Queens. She curates Brownstone Poets and edits

its annual anthology. Her latest books are *Innocence* (Finishing Line Press, 2017) and *The Cupcake Chronicles* (Poets Wear Prada, 2017).

Maria Chisolm "When I first came to Phillip's open mic, I knew it was a place I would come to on a regular basis. I liked the age group, the diversity of talents, the hours of the show and the energy level of the audience/poets. Unfortunately, I was hit by a car and couldn't come again for another six months. However, when I returned everything was still how I left it. It felt good to see the same faces and many others." Maria was born in Washington DC but raised in London and Australia. High school and College were in New York and California. Her first book was *Sudan's Angels* and she's finished a second book of poetry.

Pat Christiano "Growing up in the Bronx can limit one's perspective." As soon as Pat was old enough, he explored Manhattan and his inner landscape changed. Poetry is another kind of exploration. His first poem was an assignment in High School, a sonnet. His English teacher introduced it by saying that "this one almost makes it." That remark has bothered him ever since. Pat sees no difference between a poem and a painting. A poem is simply a wordless picture. He's sold ice to Eskimos and fruit to tourists from a stand at the foot of the Empire State Building. Now he's an artist and shows his work in Central Park.

Deborah Clapp "Becoming and being a Silver Tongued Devil makes my heart and soul "runneth" over. The Rimes show is an all-inclusive utopia. I watch, hear and feel poets' printed words spoken explode, expand and excite Truth, Beauty and so many other aspects of Love. Huge thank yous to - Phillip Giambri, Anthony Murphy, Janet Restino and C.O. Moed, the "dude" for welcoming me into this wonderful, creative "family". Coming this year for Deb – a new performance piece in honor of The Aquarian Age, a first-published collection of poems, "*Solar Woman*", and the start of a book about my grandmother, Janet Mabie. Let us all keep on together. The world needs more poetry now - more than ever!"

Lorraine LoFrese Conlin "Rimes night gave me the opportunity to be honest with the audience, read and speak without judgment, so many talents, such friendly welcoming folks, from all walks of life, all sharing and celebrating life. I grew up in Jamaica, Queens then moved to Long Island. I am still working for a global logistics company, traveling and meeting people who share my passions." Lorraine was Nassau County Poet Laureate (2015-2017) and continues hosting poetry events on Long Island.

William Considine "The hosts and crowd at "Rimes…" readings were friendly, warm and enthusiastic. And it was a crowd: arrive early if you want to sit! The readers were varied and skilled. There was always humor. Having a video of your reading afterward was a wonderful resource." Bill is originally from a mill town in the Pittsburgh area, which still looms in his poems. He studied poetry writing with Elizabeth Bishop and also writes plays. His new book, *The Furies*, is from The Operating System (2017).

Steve Dalachinsky "The energy and light-hearted mayhem that Phillip brings to every event is always inspiring and REAL. One fundamental difference between the page and stage is primarily how a piece is written and what its final intent is. Some work translates perfectly in both mediums, other poems work better on than off the page and vice versa." Born in Brooklyn after the last big war, he survived many little wars. He's been creating since he was a child, now as an elderly child, creating even more - the key to what keeps one going. He has three recent projects with two just completed and published: *Frozen Heatwave* a collaborative long poem with visual artist Yuko Otomo. *The Invisible Ray* with illustrations by Shalom Neuman (an important book on cancer) and the forthcoming *When Night and Day Become One* (the French poems - a selection 1983-2017).

Angela DiCamillo is from Southern California, moved to New York on a summer morning in 1989, and has been in love ever since. Her original intention was to be a Broadway stage actress; but realized nearly right away, that although she loved performing, it was something that she could easily walk away from; and she did with no regrets. She has been a poet and short story writer almost since she could read. She didn't take her writing seriously until her early twenties and has been writing quite consistently ever since. She hopes to one day publish a book of poetry and short stories, but for now, she continues to write and perform her work as often as she can out of pure love.

Meliora Dockery "I love the show. It's so varied and Phillip makes us performers feel like stars. I did an open mic story that was long and all he said when it eventually finished was "That was a little long." What a gentleman! Both written and spoken word should have a beginning, a middle and an end, and the protagonist should be somehow different by the end. Spoken word, while it has structure, should be extempore while printed word has to be edited and re-edited to get the precise nuance." Meliora came to the U.S. from England when she was twenty-one and within a week was featured at a storytelling show, did a skit for cable television, a photoshoot for a senior magazine, and acted in a short film. "Life is wonderful!"

Gabriel Don is the sum of many rivers, born in Paddington, Australia, taken home to Bondi Beach, Sydney. She grew up in Australia, Singapore, and Dubai and is fiercely in love with her home of ten years: The Lower East Side, New York. She's "a bunch of different things:" a filmmaker, artist, photographer, musician, and writer. Her short stories are featured in publications such as *Gargoyle 70* and her poetry collection, *Living Without Skin*, was published by A Gathering of The Tribes, Fly By Night Press.

Saara Dutton "I'm a life-long island hopper, surrounded by water on the shores of Oahu, Whidbey and now Manhattan. I've always written stories, no matter where I've lived. But

New York is where I found the courage to share them with an audience. The Rimes of The Ancient Mariner combines community spirit, Silver Tongued Devils and wayward sailors with Phillip Giambri at the helm. I also host a show, Beaver Helmet, and created a deck of tarot cards featuring our performers. There was no question which card Phillip would represent…The Hierophant: *Group energy. Community organizer. Sharing culture.* Yeah. That's about right."

Gil Fagiani (1945-2018) was a poet, translator, essayist, short-story writer, and memoirist. He has published six books of poetry of which *Missing Madonnans* (Bordighera Press, 2018) is the first posthumous and the final in a trilogy that includes *Stone Walls* and *Chianti in Connecticut*; LOGOS (Guernica Editions, 2015), *A Blanquito in El Barrio,* and *Rooks* (Rain Mountain Press); plus three chapbooks, *Crossing 116th Street, Grandpa's Wine* (Poets Wear Prada), *and Serfs of Psychiatry* (Finishing Line Press). Fagiani was a model for the late-career artist and was enjoying wider and consistent publication of his work by a variety of publishing houses when he passed away this spring after he was diagnosed with acute myeloid leukemia. Publication of his memoir, *Boogaloo Barrio* is pending as are several manuscripts he left behind including one that he collaborated on with his wife.

Jasmine Farrell "I hadn't performed for a while and was a bit nervous to be apart of the Rimes show. However, the audience and Rimes family were interactive, friendly, and supportive. I mustered up enough courage to read a poem that was snug to my heart like teddy bears to toddlers and I felt much lighter!" Jasmin is from Brooklyn, NY and has published two poetry collections. She's successfully learned "the art of brushing the mane of unicorns." She's currently working on a third poetry collection, *"Long Live Phoenixes"* and performs here and there.

Richard Fein "I'm a Brooklynite. I was devastated when the Dodgers moved. I felt betrayed. However, I recovered from that calamity. I guess this reveals my age. I've been around for quite a while, I recall reading at the Rimes show and enjoying it. But health issues have prevented me from coming more often." Richard still writes and has been published in many journals including a Wisconsin university Parallel Press chapbook series. The title is *The Required Accompanying Cover Letter (* 2011).

Duane Ferguson "I was honored to be one of the first features at Rimes of The Ancient Mariner and it was amazing. I never really considered myself a full-fledged poet until Phil blessed me with his approval. Unforgettable. Never thought about the difference between spoken and printed word. I used to say "The pen is mightier than the sword...but the tongue is the sheath from which the sword is drawn"...so I probably favor the spoken word....but words are a precious resource so no matter the vessel...we all should travel on it."

Mariposa María Teresa Fernández is an award-winning poet and author. Born and raised in the Bronx, she is a proud Puerto Rican. Her poetry has been featured on the HBO series, "Habla Ya!" and the HBO documentary "Americanos: Latino Life in the US." Mariposa has also appeared on BET, Lifetime TV, and PBS. She has performed throughout the United States, Puerto Rico, at the United Nations World Conference Against Racism, the Essence Music Festival and Black Enterprise's Women of Power Summit. Mariposa graduated from NYU with a Master's in Education and a B.A. in Women's Studies. She is the Founder and CEO of Poetry for Entrepreneurs, a business that helps entrepreneurs create messaging for their businesses through the power of poetry.

Nicole Ferraro "I had the pleasure of performing at Rimes twice: once as a booked storyteller, and once on the open mic. And I came away from both experiences feeling embraced by this thriving community of poets, storytellers, and writers, and of course the best MC of all – Philip Giambri." Nicole is still roaming the East Village and elsewhere telling stories. She's also curator and host of Art, Humanity & Action, a series that unites storytelling, activism, and fundraising.

Pauline Findlay is a poet, short story writer, and short filmmaker. Her published collection is "Mirror Images." Her second collection is "Dysfunction: a play on words in the familiar." Pauline was one of the original "Silver Tongued Devils" created by the friend she calls brother, Phillip Giambri. Her work is a stark reality recited by the characters she creates. Her poetry will leave you to ponder truths and question who we are within those scary truths we rather leave in dark corners of abandon houses. Migrating from Trinidad West Indies and being raised in America gives her a great perspective to speak from both sides of the same coin. She is also a chef at "Enoteca Maria."

Howard Finger "In my mid-twenties, I stopped writing poetry, believing I'd exhausted my creativity. I then embarked on a medical career, during which I got to know many who were living each day, uncertain that they'd see tomorrow. From these souls, I discovered what living was all about. In spite of their struggles, many still exhibited a zest for life, a thirst for knowledge and a desire to help others. The experience enlightened and inspired me. Three decades later, I began writing again—this time with a sense of purpose and an ease which would not otherwise have been possible."

Christina Fitzpatrick "I am a Libra from Massachusetts. I cannot decide whether I should write more or perform more -- or simply become a psychiatric nurse. When I was young, I thought readings were a bit masturbatory, meaning mainly for the pleasure of the writer. But after attending my first Rimes show, I realized that the spoken word can dazzle. As a matter of craft, it forces a writer to think about the audience and heightens the stakes. I've also come to realize that my voice, my delivery, and my awkwardness compliment my work."

268

Ember Flame "I loved being a part of the supportive, welcoming Rimes of the Ancient Mariner community. Though I did a poem about the long-running war I've waged on my ginger pubic hair and there were some strained silences where people were meant to laugh - so I'm not sure how well it went down!" Ember was born in Australia, spent some formative childhood years in New Zealand and was been living between Sydney and New York, her spiritual home, since 2013. Between writing letters for charities, she's dancing, writing poetry, and dreaming up new characters for her spoken word burlesque.

Kofi Fosu Forson "Thanks, Phillip Giambri, Anthony Murphy and Linda Kleinbub for making this possible. Currently, I love tweeting, trying to inspire the world a tweet at a time (Black Cocteau). One of my favorite memories as a Silver Tongued Devil was the night I sat opposite a lovely young woman I was trying to impress. During a performance by a poet I felt something moving in the back of my shirt. I reached into my shirt, grabbed at what I felt, pulled at it and threw it onto the floor. I watched as a huge water bug scampered away."

Jason Gallagher is a poet, writer, and teacher living in Northern Manhattan originally from south-central Illinois. He became involved with Rimes in the Spring of 2016 and he has always considered it THE standout performance poetry experience in New York City. He was greatly saddened by the ending of Rimes and is thrilled to be included in this anthology. Jason teaches Composition and Creative Writing at Borough of Manhattan Community College and Westchester Community College. He lives with his wife, fellow poet, Brendaliz Guerrero-Gallagher and their rat terrier Frida.

Art Gatti "I have loved bathing my senses in the polyglot experiences at Rimes-- laughed, cried, raged. I'm still getting over my college (1964) aversions to spoken word poetry, but I think that my interim performance experiences (theater, song, comedy) are slowly curing me of that." Art is a Queens refugee, panhandled nickels to buy Thunderbird wine in Newark in '66 and organized with SDS there. He's currently exploring new ways of haiku-ing the universe. See: *Lonely Planet Haiku and Senryu* on Facebook and translating for Spanish/English poetry pubs, *DarkLight*.

Jennifer Harmon Gersbeck is a poet born and raised in New Mexico and currently residing in Astoria, Queens. Inspired by her late mother Patty, also a writer, Jennifer's goal is to share their story with the world. Her work is heavily influenced by personal relationships with family and friends as well as the atmosphere of the Southwest desert and the East Coast. Although she misses the hot enchiladas and the enchanting pastel pink and orange sunsets of New Mexico, she has formed a rich and rewarding life in New York City. Intertwining her mother's writings with her own, Jennifer's poetry readings provide a unique and often very moving experience to her audience.

Vogue Giambri "Phillip always introduces me as the younger better looking Giambri. But we all know it's not true, he's way better looking. Have you seen his tats? Silver

Tongue Devil readings changed my life. Poetry has been the avenue into becoming the creative I am today. Poetry came first. I'm grateful that I have been able to feel a part of the long rich history of spoken word in the heart of New York City." Vogue is a writer, director, poet, and photographer currently based in London.

Robert Gibbons "I think the Silver Tongue reading series is an important part of our community. Phillip has participated in many of the readings around the East and West Village. I appreciate him and the series for giving me the opportunity to read and feature." Three Rooms Press published Robert's first poetry collection, *Close to the Tree* in 2012. He's completing his MFA at City College in Creative Writing this semester and is considering art school. He loves writing ekphrastic poems and takes classes every Saturday at the Arts Students League in Manhattan. He loves the journey. His dream is to one day travel the world, write, support, and collect art.

Gordon A Gilbert Jr. "Featuring at Rimes in front of Phillip and many fellow writers was great in itself, but I also got a limited-edition Silver Tongued Devil -shirt!" A long-time NYC west villager, Gordon performs poetry, songs, and monologues in the metropolitan area. He's also written short stories and a play, *Monologues from the Old Folks Home*, produced seven times at NYC venues. He's hosted many NYC poetry readings celebrating famous poets and writers (especially the Beat Generation) and for some years has also curated a "Remembrances of 9/11" reading every September.

Joel Louis Gold is an Improvisational Spoken Word Artist, writer, director, and Director of Photography. He's also a film and video artist who has won numerous awards for his work. Joel was the first recipient of a Guggenheim Fellowship in video and received an Emmy for his work in film. He's worked on disparate projects including dance, music, drama, and fashion. He's been performing spoken word for a lifetime and improvisational spoken word remains his ART.

Russ Green is a graduate of Hofstra University. His work has appeared in a variety of publications. He has read from Santa Fe to the belly of the polar vortex in Cleveland, to the ghost of Kerouac in Lowell, Massachusetts. Russ is co-editor at Great Weather for Media. He runs Green's Revolution poetry series in Amityville, Long Island and a quarterly series at the Brickhouse Brewery in Patchogue, NY. Trekking the Himalayas, wandering through Europe, driving across America, communicating with the Green Mountains of Vermont. He lives in Setauket, NY with a tuxedo cat and a rice maker.

Christopher Grigsby "The spoken word is both ephemeral and eternal. Eternal, because it preceded any form of writing and carries meaning upon meaning overlaid in overtones that rise beyond the vocabulary itself. Ephemeral, because for most of history, the spoken word was fated to vanish instantly. I see my written words primarily as a script for spoken performance, but recognize the page as an essential blueprint. The blueprint charts the underlying territory, while the performance is the transformative fire through which the written words rise to resonate as living experience. The book is open to read. Transform the words as you please."

Brendaliz Guerrero is a New York native Afro-Latina born and raised in Washington Heights. Her chosen method of expression is a delicious marriage of spoken and written/printed word. While performed pieces are an exhilarating experience, she's fascinated by simply reading off a page or screen and letting the visual text paint the image in her mind. Poetry is her canvas and story-telling is her paintbrush. Lately, however, Brendaliz is being inspired by married life with fellow poet Jason Gallagher-Guerrero and their seven-year-old rat terrier Frida, named after artist Frida Kahlo.

John S. Hall "I grew up in Manhattan, where I still live. I love Rimes -it reminds me of the first open readings I went to in the mid-'80s in the Village (Speakeasy, The Back Fence)…I've always thought my work sounds better than it reads." John has three active bands where he performs his spoken word stuff: *Unusual Squirrel* released recordings in 2017 and he'll probably record *Invisible Dog* in 2018. *Sensation Play*, a concept band about sex and male submission, will also be recorded in 2018. *King Missile* was active in the 1990's and performs live occasionally.

L. R. Laverde Hansen "Many things in New York are unreliable. Subway trains break down, jobs fall through, and significant others break up with you. Once a month, just about everybody can have a chance to express their artistic side at the Rimes show. Hosted by the Ancient Mariner himself, it is where I have felt my most satisfying moments as a writer and artist. Being a Silver Tongued Devil has connected me to a community of downtown artists, I admire how I am simply left to perform as I wish. The Mariner reiterates at the beginning of every Rimes event, this is your space, your time, your world. Sometimes that has given license for the ridiculous and the absurd, but who am I to say, my work is not ridiculous or absurd?"

Holly Hepp-Galvan "So proud to be a Silver Tongued Devil and to join the rapid-fire voices in the Three of Cups Lounge! Performing poetry is about being present and wild in the moment and also about being part of an ancient tradition. In my secret heart, I'm a roving wordsmith, a bindlestiff bard, a rappin' rhythmist that ridicules the system. I love the language and the beat, the rhythm, and recurrence. During the days I write plays and make puppets for the stage. I also teach college courses to all new authors."

Judith Lee Herbert ""She's making me cry!" Phillip exclaimed after I read at an open mic at Rimes, and then he invited me to be a featured reader. His warmth, enthusiasm, respect, and authenticity has provided a supportive environment to me and all the poets in the Rimes community. As a feature, I experienced not only Phillip's enthusiastic support, but also his ability to structure readings, and to run the evening's program like a tight ship. He generously records every reader for YouTube, and provides each person with a gift, not only of the reading that evening, but also a lasting memento."

Ann Herendeen "Brooklyn forever. I (type)write because it's something creative I can do with my deformed hands, deliverance from the starvation diet, sawdust and sand, of housework and daily tasks. Writing for spoken word is more fun than writing for print alone. (Thank you, Ancient Mariner!) It's a different sound in the mind, even if it starts with the same process of silent composition. Sometimes what I have to say won't fit into a five-minute slot, and I have to write long. Am hoping to complete my current project, *The Anger Bomb*, before I die."

Blair Hopkins "The Rimes show is unique in its unpretentious atmosphere. It attracts a fascinating array of participants and experience levels. For my first (ever!) reading, Phillip and I co-read a piece we wrote together: "Are You Dangerous?". I'm grateful to Rimes for reigniting my interest in writing; prior, I hadn't written anything with intent in years. I moved to NYC in 2009 and work as a freelance photographer specializing in events and portraiture. My first book, *All In A Day's [Sex] Work*, is a photojournalistic exploration into the daily lives of sex workers."

Vicki Iorio "I am a proud Silver Tongued Devil. I performed in the *What The Hell is Love* project and *Barflies and Broken Angels*. The best part of the shows is meeting all the poets, putting a face to their words. I have a love/hate relationship with spoken vs. printed word. I love to perform my work and feel compelled to shock and awe. I just hope these pieces shock the printed page as well." Vicki is a Long Island native currently living in Florida trees. Her chapbook, *Something Fishy*, will be published by Finishing Line Press in late summer, 2018.

Jerry T. Johnson is a Poet and Spoken Word Artist whose poetry has appeared in a variety of literary journals. Jerry features at many spoken word venues in the New York City and Connecticut areas. He grew up in South Carolina where he lived until his late thirties. After living in Central Europe and Russia for years, Jerry returned to the USA and currently lives in Danbury, Connecticut with his wife Raye. It was in Danbury that Jerry picked up his writing pen after a twenty-three-year hiatus. Having both featured at Rimes of the Ancient Mariner and participated in several Rimes open mics, Jerry appreciates the vibe and atmosphere generated by the Rimes poetry events.

Boni Joi "I met the AM at the We Three Telephone Bar Series. Later I read for Rimes and it was a delightful experience since I also have a long history with Three of Cups. I was born in Dance, spent my childhood in Surrealism and currently live in Dada, Switzerland. When composing a poem, I think about how it visually looks and reads on the page, however, I also love the sound of words and after writing a line down I read it out loud, and then edit accordingly. Currently working on my second collection, working title *The Information Game*, and a series of poems based on 125 paintings by Paul Klee."

272

Jennifer Juneau is the author of the full-length poetry collection, "*More Than Moon*," by Is a Rose Press and the novel "*ÜberChef USA*," a satire on reality TV, by Spork Press. Her work has been twice nominated for the Pushcart Prize in fiction, the Million Writers Award and a Sundress Best of the Net and has appeared in the Brownstone Anthology, Cafe Review, Cincinnati Review, Columbia Journal, Evergreen Review, GWFM, Live Mag!, Local Knowledge, Seattle Review, Sensitive Skin Magazine and elsewhere. She is currently working on a new poetry collection called "*Night of the Manhattans*" and a second novel called "*The Rock Star and the Girls Who Loved Him.*"

Qurrat Ann Kadwani "Meeting Phillip Giambri is something that I'm so grateful for. We met at an open mic, and he supported me when my solo play *They Call Me Q* was produced at several venues including Off-Broadway. He invited me to be a Silver Tongued Devil. I was impressed by the variety of work presented and I remember that I wrote something specifically for the show. Re-watching it now, it was definitely "experimental," but that is the freedom that Phillip gives - to be a devil with words! Phillip was the first person to read my new solo play *Intrusion*, and his candid, constructive notes made me work harder to create a product that I am now so proud to tour!"

Linda Kleinbub "I was new to the spoken word scene when I discovered the Rimes show. Phillip really cared about his audience. No matter how nervous or scared you were, he made everyone feel welcome." Linda is a native New Yorker who received her MFA from The New School, she co-hosts the monthly Fahrenheit Open Mic. Her work has appeared in *The New York Observer, The Brooklyn Rail, The Best American Poetry Blog, and Yahoo! Beauty.* Her first full-length book of poetry is forthcoming from A Gathering of the Tribes / Fly By Night Press.

Ron Kolm "I have had the great honor of reading in Phillip Giambri's Rimes series at the Three of Cups many times over the years. I value his friendship greatly. I also value the videos he shot as you performed there. Watching them on YouTube gave me a chance to 'proof' my work. I would try to change words I stumbled over while reading – they almost always turned out to have simply been wrong – and getting rid of them made the pieces better. My new book, *A Change in the Weather*, benefited from this process. Thank you so much for everything, Phillip!"

Ptr Kozlowski "My great-great-granddaddy wasn't exactly a mariner but he worked the oyster boats on Long Island Sound. He may have sung sea shanties in the 1880s and I was in a New Wave band in the 1980s. He knew a red sky at night is a sailor's delight and I know so is the Three of Cups. Down below where the rum and the tales can flow. Like Phillip, I've taken as my spyglass a video cam."

Wayne Kral is a collage artist and writer who has lived in and been inspired by the LES for the last thirty years. For twenty of those years, he co-produced a reading series and hosted numerous open mics in the LES. He has participated in group shows in NYC, SF, and Lisbon, Portugal.

Beth Corliss Lamont bills herself as a wilted Flower Child from San Fran, who was privileged to walk across the Golden Gate Bridge at its Ribbon Cutting in 1937. "Make Love, not war!" This is the Peace-loving mantra that must prevail! Beth is a Chaplain who promotes "Humanist Healing" for the Woes of the World! Holding hope that we are still evolving into wiser beings, she advocates practicing the 3-Rs: not "readin'-ritin'-n'rithmetic," But, instead: Reason, Respect and Responsibility! Do your best here and now! Let hereafter take care of itself! Beth is the author of "Lefties Are In Their Right Minds!" She Sends Humanist Hugs!

Jean Le Bec "I was born and have lived in Brooklyn my entire life. I have always told stories. As an elementary school teacher, telling stories about my life to the children I taught was a way to give them the freedom to tell their own stories. I loved performing *Butterfly Kiss* at Rimes of The Ancient Mariner. This show is such a wonderful opportunity for artists of both the written word and spoken word to come together." Jean is a Moth story slam winner and for the past five years has been telling stories extensively throughout NYC.

Jane LeCroy "My first Silver Tongued Devil experience was *Barflies and Broken Angels*. I was hooked! Spoken Word and the page are each different literary mediums that transcend language through the subtle limitations of each of their parameters." In addition to publishing, Jane has two performance projects that express her poetry: her band **The Icebergs**, vox/cello/drums, has the CD *Eldorad*" and, an improvisational music project centered around a modular synth and a mix of other

instruments, $\Omega \nabla$ **(Ohmslice)** which has the vinyl "*Conduit*", both on Imaginator Records.

Linda Lerner "I'm a Brooklyn native, and live in Carroll Gardens where I've lived since moving out of Lower Manhattan in 2001, three weeks after the attack on the WTC. Charlie Parker said, "If you don't live it, it won't come out your horn," or I might add play on the page, which is what's been happening at Three of Cups every month since Phil Giambri created this all-inclusive, non- judgmental monthly event; it's what I love about it. I write as I think out of an urban sensibility. *Taking the F train* is forthcoming from NYQ Books.*"

Karen Levy "I had no idea I was going to a dive bar to read, so I brought my 12-year-old, and what a cast of characters! Wild and wacky and wondrous with words, tried and true to the venue, and true to Philip, too, the Ancient Mariner, a dream of a host, loving us all and urging us on. His magic made me feel welcome and wanted once I stepped on stage, and so, a remarkable crew of poets and writers, storytellers and speakers, thinkers and stinkers return, time again, to this dive; all of them, all of us, feeling we've come home."

274

Maria Lisella is the first Italian American Queens Poet Laureate. Her Pushcart Prize-nominated work appears in *Thieves in the Family* (NYQ Books), *Amore on Hope Street* (Finishing Line Press) and *Two Naked Feet* (Poets Wear Prada). Her work has appeared in *LIPS, Shrew, New Verse News, The New York Quarterly, Skidrow Penthouse, Paterson Literary Revie and Ovunque Siamo,* in anthologies T*he Traveler's Vade Mecum* (Red Hen Press, 2017.) Her essay, *Shades, Colors and Internal Dialogues* appears in *What Does It Mean to Be White in America?* (2LeafPress) her travel piece, *Lemmings* appears in the five-volume collection *She Can Find Her Way* (Upper Hand Press, 2017). She curates the twenty-eight-year-old Italian American Writers Association literary series.

"Big Fuckin' Mike" Logan always tries to get up on stage first, especially at the Rimes of the Ancient Mariner reading series. "When first bursting upon the downtown poetry scene in July 1998..? Considered myself to be a writer who reads my own material, on-stage...Now...? These many years later...? Discovered that I was an entertainer, a performer who wrote his own material! Are you not entertained...? Current Reigning King Neptune @ The 37th Annual Coney Island Mermaid Parade, and appearing late night on the Manhattan Neighborhood Network /MNN on the live Variety Show: "Brane Kandy," Tuesdays @ 10:30 pm MNN2/Channel 56."

Michael Lydon "I met Phillip Giambri a few years ago and we hit it off right away. I admire his dedication to writing as an art that everyone can share. He's smart, funny, and has a deeply sympathetic soul. Every time we run into each other on the spoken word/music circuit, I'm glad to see him. Writing, which I love, begins with speech. If it sounds good, most often it reads well. I'm a Boston Irish kid, have loved writing ever since I was in the first grade. Music came along later. I love combining words and notes. Right now I'm editing a new book, *Busy Being Born*, a memoir of the 60s."

Jenna Lynch is a poet and professor living in Astoria, Queens. She works as the Reading and Writing Specialist at Fairleigh Dickinson University and also teaches a creative writing workshop for teens at SUNY Purchase. Jenna's work has appeared in Sundog Lit, Construction Magazine, Forklift, Ohio, among others. Her chapbook, *The Mouth of Which You Are,* is forthcoming from Finishing Line Press.

Taylor Mali A twelfth-generation resident of New Amsterdam (later Manhattan), Mali is the founding curator of the Page Meets Stage reading series at the Bowery Poetry Club and the inventor of Metaphor Dice, a creative writing aid that will make writing a poem so easy he will soon be out of a job.

Peter Marra "Featuring twice at Rimes are two memories I will always hold dear to my heart. Since I write fairly transgressive pieces, I've been touched by the warmth and acceptance I've received. It's a truly unique and impressive gathering of widely divergent personalities. I was born in Brooklyn, ran away to the East Village and Times Square in the 70's and 80's ran around with devils and angels, now I'm here." Peter's new book of poetry due out in June 2018 is, "*Random Acts of Violence*". His psycho-sexual-giallo novel *A Naked Kiss From a Broken Doll* is due out in December 2018.

C. O. Moed "I was at a point where either I reclaimed my work or jumped off a ledge. The second I stepped on stage at Phil's open mic, I stepped off ledges. Saying things out loud on stage breaks open my emotional prison and I see how my story is other peoples' story too. It's fucking great. Grew up on NY's Lower East Side when it was still a tough neighborhood. *It Was Her New York*: stories on a disappearing family and fading city. Upcoming – *This Highspeed Mess Called Life*: illustrated pieces about relationships, family and the MTA. - Also, some sex."

Anthony Moscini "A friend gave me a book of e.e. cummings some years back when I was a struggling actor. This book of poetry caused a great shift in my ambitions, causing me to begin writing, about twenty-five years ago. In addition to doing poetry readings, I have facilitated a weekly poetry group at the Riverside Library and been grateful to appear as a featured poet and Silver Tongued Devil for the Rimes of The Ancient Mariner series, a miracle of poetry. I have also had several poems appear in various editions of the Riverside Poets Anthology and was selected as the featured poet at Rogue'sScholars.com."

Anthony C. Murphy "I've been here since Rimes Day One, although not ever-present. Phil asked me to be a part of his adventure so I came on board. I have seen most of the contributors to this anthology read their stuff out loud more than twice. It's eclectic. The spoken word is less ambiguous than the written. You see emphasis through nuance in a good reader. We all love a good storyteller. I'm from Lancashire but my dad was Irish. Jokes, tall tales, gossip and ghost stories were what we traded in. Some can captivate with that. I'm writing a book about it. Go figure."

Arthur Nersesian was born and raised in Manhattan. His grandfather was born on 8th Street & Avenue B in 1898, and throughout the last thirty-eight years he's lived only a few blocks from there. He is the author of ***The Fuck-Up***, about the East Village in the 1980s. He has also written ten other novels, most set in or around the neighborhood. He was Managing Editor of *The Portable Lower East Side*, a cultural journal that was defunded by Jesse Helms in the 1990s. For the past four years, he has run the affordable East Village Writer's Workshop, which meets every Monday night year-round. Anyone interested in joining is more than welcome to contact him via Facebook.

Kurt Nelson Peloquin aka Nelson Quin is a spoken word artist, songwriter, and multimedia producer residing in Bushwick Brooklyn. Over the past ten years, he has helped organizations like Humans Rights Watch, Microsoft, The Pediatric Cancer Research Foundation, and many more, tell their stories through film and shared experiences. For the past year, he has focused on developing his art and sharing inspirational messages of hope and love amidst the fear and hatred of our times. He has performed as a featured artist at The Inspired Word NYC, hosted an empowerment workshop with Big Brothers Big Sisters, and is extremely grateful for the opportunity to grace the stage at Rimes of The Ancient Mariner.

Puma Perl "Phillip Giambri's series provided an appreciative host and an attentive audience, which stand out more to me than anything I did during my features or open mic readings. I also thought it was great that he took the time to record everyone." Puma Perl is a lifelong New Yorker, born and bred, still lives on the Lower East Side. Since 2012, she's produced, hosted and curated Puma Perl's Pandemonium, at the Bowery Electric, merging poetry with rock and roll. Her upcoming book, *"Birthdays Before and After,"* published by Beyond Baroque Press, will be her fifth solo collection.

Begonya Plaza "By chance, I met Philip Giambri one sunny afternoon in Grassroots Tavern. I ordered a Jameson and sat back to relish the memories of a time in the eighties when I used to live in the area as a young struggling performer/storyteller. Phillip walked in and headed straight over to my side of the bar. He sat down and subtly mentioned that he usually sits in my stool. I answered I can understand why, it's the best stool in the house. We then quickly got to talking about old times, realizing just how much we had in common and how real the other was. I fell in love with Phillip's wild energy and juicy imagination. So when he invited me to come share some poetry at his Rimes reading, I accepted. With Phillip, it's about provoking truth and pushing the artistic envelope in this screwy mercantile world. Cheers!"

Vincent Quatroche Born on the end of the North Fork of Long Island in the mid 50's estranged native son Vincent Quatroche was banished from the Island in the 70s due to lack of conspicuous consumption of consumer products. Vincent Quatroche is currently a journeyman educator/irritant de jour teaching in the Communication Department at SUNY Fredonia in Western New York. He has been publishing in book, audio and video formats for the past thirty years which has been widely distributed and largely ignored in the US & abroad. A recent collection *Seeing Eye Ear* was released 12/2017 in digital format on CD Baby.

Rivke Lela Reid "The Silver Tongued Devil that never was: the venue closed days before my night. The works presented before were "on the page", that is, seeing words and layout were part of the act. For my cancelled debut, I created a fugal vocal work, designed as "spoken word". Never did self-produce a video of it. I typically do sound composition, play clavichord, and write provocative essays. From 2014-2017, a poet's voice emerged during a triple crisis informed by gender rage. The rage has moved on. As have I, to Belchertown, MA. Great writers' groups and yummy produce!"

Janet Restino Visual artist/word artist/etc. "Somehow, I became part of the Giambri Rimes Gang - I wanted a good hang, filled in as House Manager when Russell Atwood left town. It's a good trip working with Phillip and Murph where I can spew forth my fountain of words to open ears and minds in drinking sinking basements in the East Village, one of my old home-sweet-homes. Makes up for having to grow up in a culture of repressive family values enabled by Catholic indoctrination forcing me to be silent for way too long. Well that's all over now, isn't it!!! Hear ye hear ye! Glad to be here in this Rimes Anthology."

Stan Rifken "I began doing comedy monologues, in the summer of 1978, in Washington Square Park. When the weather got cold, I began hitting the clubs. In those days the city was awash in open-mic venues. For the price of a beer, and the willingness to sit through the acts of everyone else in the room, you could present your material. After every show, my father would ask me "So, is this going to lead to anything?" Forty years later, I know the answer. It has led to a life of creativity and mindful existence. Which is why we're all here."

Joe Roarty "i always found th rimes xperience 2 b an xciting hi-nrg affair-both 4 myself & th performances i witnessd-i hav poetizd n filly,chgo, & a few othr places & rimes was as ntns as anything i evr saw-i will miss it"

Stephanie Rogers "Being a Silver Tongued Devil was an unexpected gift that reminded me why Spoken Word will always have my heart. At the risk of sounding like a romantic (or mad scientist), the Written Word is like building a new being, making sure all the parts fit. But standing at the microphone and sharing with fellow storytellers and poets breathes life into the words, and myself as well." Stephanie is a lifelong native of Queens, NY currently piecing together two chapbooks with the encouragement of her new husband.

Jeff Rose is an author, storyteller, showrunner, and podcast producer living in Brooklyn. He wrote this flash piece for a Rimes show in 2017 and felt flattered when he was asked if it was true. (It isn't.) *Flavor* is dedicated to the memory of Dr. Michael Abott.

Marie A. Sabatino "Glad to be a part of this collection. The Silver Tongued Devil anthology is not only making history but preserving it. When I heard the home of the Rimes of The Ancient Mariner show (Three of Cups Lounge) closed its doors after over twenty-five years of serving and taking in the East Village community from all walks of life - including me and my friends, the men in my life who have come and gone, and even my dogs - it felt like the perfect time to hold on to this slice of New York City between our fingers for just a little bit longer."

LinDel Sandlin A recovering Southern Baptist, she writes poems exploring politics, religion, Mother Nature and misadventures in love. "I was delighted when Phillip

278

dubbed me one of his Silver Tongued Devils and shocked to learn that made me part of NYC's underground spoken word artists. NO ONE did what Phillip did - recorded every single show, edited the videos and posted them individually to YouTube. Coming from an acting background, my poems are particularly better suited for spoken word performance. The inflections, body language, humorous tone for heavy subjects, do not translate to the page anywhere close to that of experiencing it in the audience. Thanks largely to Phillip, you can watch me on YouTube."

Christine Santelli has been on the NYC music scene for more than twenty-five years. A Blues Hall of Fame Inductee and songwriter for Grammy-nominated album *"Worthy"*, Santelli is not new to the written word, she has been writing songs and lyrics for decades. "*Dragonfly*," Santelli's eighth CD, continues to burnish her reputation as a critically respected artist with that much sought-after quality—street cred. "…Christine Santelli's solo acoustic stunner Dragonfly is a complex, coming of age work…the matured singer-songwriter whose voice and acoustic guitar alone give wings to her poetry." Dave McGee.

Erica Schreiner is an experimental video artist, performance artist and writer, living and working in NYC. She's certain of nothing.

Michael Schwartz was born with Coney Island complications, including a forked tongue. After a lifetime of sub-lingual longings, his linguine was ready to be dipped in silver marinara by the Ancient Mariner at Three of Cups East Village Pasta and Pizzeria. The pickled-ink pontiff pitched Schwartz's fork, ordaining him a devil of the dungeon where haunted souls chant their smells and conjugate their tomatoes in the bubbling cauldron. But then the high priests of real estate padlocked the gate, so Schwartz joins the exorcism of their rent-raising gentrification pathology, with a dead-raising publication entitled *The Silver Tongued Devil Anthology*.

Yuyutsu RD Sharma an internationally acclaimed South Asian poet and translator, has published nine poetry collections including, *Eternal Snow: A Worldwide Anthology of One Hundred Twenty-Five Poetic Intersections with Himalayan Poet Yuyutsu RD Sharma (*David B. Austell- Editor, Kathleen D. Gallagher- Editor, 2017*) A Blizzard in my Bones: New York Poems* (Nirala, 2016), *Quaking Cantos: Nepal Earthquake Poems*, (Nirala, 2016), *Milarepa's Bones, 33 New Poems*, (Nirala, 2012), *Nepal Trilogy, Photographs and Poetry on Annapurna, Everest, Helambu & Langtang*, (Epsilonmedia, Karlsruhe, 2010 with renowned German photographer Andreas Stimm), *Space Cake, Amsterdam, & Other Poems from Europe and America*, (2009, Indian reprint 2014) and Annapurna Poems, 2008, Reprint, 2012).

Verandah-Maureen Shepard is Brooklyn native, currently residing in San Antonio, Texas. Serving as Assistant Principal at IDEA Mays Academy, she's been an educator for almost a decade sharing her love of learning and the arts with underserved kids and their families. "Spoken word is lyrical, raw, transformative, vulnerable. I prefer to perform, always. A memorable performance is as a Silver Tongued Devil. Warm and receptive audiences, phenomenal artist energy on any given lineup—it's magic." "*Suite Life*", a conceptual three-part album is her newest project. Two of its singles have been released and can be found on her website.

Edmund Siejka "Poet, playwright, actor. Two poetry collections, three plays and more TV parts than I care to remember. Yes, I do that. But along the way, I met good people who encouraged me. Phillip Giambri welcomed everyone, the Village hipsters, working people, people looking for work and those artists whose voices need to be heard. His venue was the Three of Cups and he greeted everyone to the big tent known as Rimes of The Ancient Mariner. With his support poets brought words to life and for a few hours, the audience witnessed the ordinary transformed into magic."

Melanie Sirof "Brooklyn born, Long Island raised, molded by the mountains of Boulder, Colorado, a high school teacher by day, poet by night. I watch the die-hard Rime's returnees and the Devils who take the stage, and think *yes, exactly*. They are the greatest of storytellers and the most fascinating of people. Grateful to be counted among them. Thank you, Phillip, for the invite into the underground world of poetry that continues to exist in NYC, and for laughing (loudly) at all the right moments."

Chloe' Skye is a poet, ESL teacher, and travel blogger at *Chlohemian*. There are three places she's most at home: the American Northeast, Israel, and the Czech Republic; she has been living in the latter for four years. Endlessly curious and a lover of language, when she started performing on stage in 2014 it coincided with the decision to move abroad. She believes speaking poetry gives different life to the written word and voice to the poet. During her Rimes feature, she was nervous, nervous, nervous!... until she suddenly started owning it.

Moira T. Smith
"*Who am I?* I'm a Watcher, sharing my observations regarding the drama and absurdity of this human trip.
Spoken vs written word: Within the context of oral tradition, the spoken word outlasts the written word, by a long-shot. Hence, the written word should be carved into stone whenever possible.
Current projects: If I printed out and stacked up all my work, the pile would be ten feet high. That's a lot of carving, yo.
The upshot: Phillip is the reason that *Rimes* is a worthwhile gathering, plain and simple. Its success is a reflection of his love and generosity. Props!!"

Coree Spencer hails from a small town in Massachusetts, went to college in Athens, Georgia and has spent almost thirty years in New York City. She's enjoyed taking part in many spoken word venues in the East Village and Lower East Side and is grateful to be a

Silver Tongued Devil! Her stories are on some literary websites including, DUCTS.org, Mr. Beller's Neighborhood, and Sensitive Skin. She is currently working on the memoir, *American Refugees*, an account of her family's teacher exchange experience in a small English village in 1974.

Peter Sragher b. 1960, Bucharest, Romania. B.A. in German and English at Bucharest University. President of Bucharest Branch-Literary Translations of the Romanian Writers' Union. Poetry collections: *I am the dragon*, China Renmin University Press, Beijing, 2019, *Akropolis – the Ascension*, Athens, 2019; Peter Sragher /Claus Ankersen, I*n Defense of the Cherries*, Timişoara, 2019. Prose: C*artea Lui David (The Book of David)*, Timişoara, 2017. Poetry translations: *Bernhard Widder, Ernst David, Gerhard Kofler, Bruno Weinhals & Christian Loidl* (in bilingual editions*)*. Photo exhibitions: *Living Wood, Broken Wood, Dead Wood* in Prater & Lobau – Austria, Bucharest, 2007. Coordinator: Monthly *Review of Literary Translations*.

Zev Torres "Around the time I began attending poetry readings, I learned that I prefer the thrill of reciting my work from memory. When I choose a piece for a reading, my intention is not to simply revisit something that I wrote, but to experience its relevance in the moment while allowing the moment to become part of the piece -- be it in the form of a different phrase or a shift in emphasis. Untethering my eye from the written word allows me to reconnect with the creative spirit that infused the piece at its inception."

John J. Trause was exhilarated attending/participating in Rimes readings as audience member/open mic performer before featuring as a Silver Tongued Devil and hanging out with Phil, Murph, and Janet at the bar close to closing. Gives it all on both page and stage, ink and mic. Born: Teaneck, NJ. Grew up and lives: Wood-Ridge, NJ. Studied with Homer, Sappho, Catullus, and Virgil. Kicked Eratosthenes's ass in wrestling, but kissed Callimachus's. Worked in four great libraries, including the Museum of Modern Art Library, NYC, and is now Director of the Oradell Public Library. Engaged in three ekphrastic projects already in 2017. Procrastinates on other lit shit.

John Trigonis "Being a Silver Tongued Devil and sharing the stage with extraordinary poetic talent and personalities has been the comeback I needed after my ten-year stint as a filmmaker." John hails from Jersey City, NJ, and has been performing poetry since the age of eighteen. Right now, he feels like he's starting from scratch again, but he's hoping his upcoming chapbook, *Growing Pains* will showcase the best poems written during his absence from the open mic and poetry scenes.

Anoek van Praag "The Rimes Family has given me a place "where everybody knows your name." It is the most welcoming, supportive and physically pleasing place to read poetry in New York that I have seen." Anoek has always written poetry as a performance piece, which brings life to words and meaning. She also simply loves doing it!! She's from The Netherlands, hence her expansive knowledge of languages. Anoek started writing as a teenager and never stopped. Her writing is colored by her background - post-war Europe - and through much grief and loss, morphed into joy and love. She works as a Tantric Educator, Intimacy Counselor and works with trauma and PTSD, helping people overcome issues dealing with intimacy, sensuality, and sexuality. Anoek believes "we live from our senses," even though we think we live from our heads!

Angelo Verga "I'm both Jewish and Sicilian; a born and bred New Yorker. I remember everything; am volatile; and, yes, I do think I own the street." *Long & Short, the Street in Your Head*, is the most recent of his seven books of poems and is available on Amazon. He lives in Harlem, not far from where he was born.

Margarette Wahl is from Massapequa Long Island. Rimes of The Ancient Mariner readings were her first experiences reading her poetry in NYC. She'll never forget how her poem: *He Lives On,* a tribute to the late Robin Williams, won over the city audience one-night reading as a Silver Tongued Devil. Margarette is published in a number of Anthologies and has two chapbooks with Local Gems Press. She is the co-host of a Performance Poets Association poetry reading at the Bellmore Bean Cafe every third Monday of the month.

George Wallace is a third-generation New Yorker building on the heritage of an immigrant working-class family whose second generation contributed to the vitality of NYC's mid-century haute couture and popular performing arts scenes. He's lived widely around the US, Europe, Asia as a hippy traveler, a health care worker, and a performing poet. George organized regional poetry communities around NYC while growing his own art, with particular focus on Beat, Surrealist and Poet Maudit traditions. These days he represents the Walt Whitman Birthplace as writer-in-residence.

Robert Watlington is a native New York artist and writer born in Harlem who's spent his adult life in the West and East Village. Bobby started creating before seriously considering whether what he produced was art. Having been exposed to some of the best artists in the world in the East Village during the sixties, seventies, and eighties, he observed and learned from them. He paints to express inner emotions and feelings through abstract colors. "Phillip's handling of his former poetry readings was a top-shelf presentation that was professionally run. I rarely got involved in open mic readings. I prefer listening to others. Phillip and company, past and present, have restored my interest in the poetry scene."

Eytan Stern Weber "I knew I loved Rimes after my first open mic. Of course, everyone was exceptionally welcoming, and even though anyone could perform, the standard of talent was better than any other mic I'd been to. But what made me love Rimes was that it made me feel naïve. People of all ages, from all walks of life, each with a unique voice, speaking so passionately honestly made me realize that my work was missing that raw emotion. Ever since then, with every new piece I've written, I've asked myself if it would stand up to the caliber of Rimes."

Susan Weiman "After reading *Roommates,* my short fiction pieces, at Three of Cups, people would approach me, and tell their roommate stories. I've become an expert. A roommate consultant. A roommate therapist. *"Yes, you do have to kiss 100 frogs to find a roommate. My advice: keep kissing and ask the essential questions. If you don't, you will find out anyway." (From Roommates)."*

Francine Witte "I loved being a Silver Tongued Devil. Great audience. Cool setting. And whatta host! He puts you on YouTube. I love both printed and spoken word but in different ways. Sometimes you want to be alone with a really beautiful thought and let it slowly unfold itself to you and other times, you want to be entertained and become part of a performance." Francine grew up in Queens, lived in Vermont and Buffalo, but came back to New York and loves it here. "So much to do all the time. I'm working on flash fiction and more poetry."

Mickey Wyte was raised in Brooklyn. Drafted in '68, he served a tour of duty as a Combat Infantryman in Vietnam. **"**I became a Silver Tongue Devil when my buddy Phil Giambri—*the most interesting man in the world*— gave me the opportunity to perform at Identity Bar in the East Village. It was a memorable time for me, having my grown daughter sitting in the front row." Mickey's currently working on a collection of short stories based on his experience in Viet Nam. His hard-boiled mystery novel, *A Fashion to Kill*, is available on Amazon.

Anton Yakovlev is Russian but is extremely bad at programming, let alone hacking, is too antisocial to collude with anyone, and has never looked into Vladimir Putin's eyes. His latest poetry collection is *Ordinary Impalers* (Kelsay Books, 2017). He has also written and directed several short films, including *12 Scenes From a Relationship*, in which he had a cameo as Antichrist Porphyro, Archbishop of the Second Satanic Church of Baltimore.

Susan Yung After graduating College, Susan became a Chinatown activist via the Basement Workshop, Seven Loaves, Charas, Nuyorican Poets Café, City Arts, Asian American Arts Alliance, A Gathering of the Tribes, Spring Studio and finally attending open mics in the Lower East Side. By 1979 she became a freelance typesetter, saved some money and eventually traveled around to Third World nations as a photographer. Tiring of still images, she later moved on to video where for twenty years she documented LES alternative jazz musicians. i.e. Billy Bang, Ras Moshe Burnett, Jemeel Moondoc, Will Connell, Jr, Butch Morris, David Hammons, Larry Roland, Steve Swell, Roy Campbell, Kali Fasteau, and many more.

Nick Zaharakos "My passions are writing short stories, telling tales, and cooking. I use the same ingredients for all three; memory and imagination. Memory helps me preserve people, events, places, feelings, and recipes that I want to perfect. Imagination serves to explore uncharted territories, unique philosophies, and new recipes. I am grateful that Rimes gives a variety of performers a platform." Nick's universe lies in his East Flatbush, Brooklyn childhood. He was the middle of seven children living with grandparents along with Mom and Pop in a small railroad flat. They were the only family of Greek immigrants in the neighborhood. He is a Vietnam Combat Veteran and lived the single life in Manhattan until his marriage to Joann.

Alana Zonan "Spoken word poetry has allowed me to express my pondering in a voice and cadence that I control in a way that printed word has never really allowed me. Being a Silver Tongued Devil provides a platform, a stage for me and so many other artists to let those voices be heard. The energy is quintessential New York City and I identify with this immensely. Nowadays you'll find me producing commercials and short films which can be found on my website and my poetry popping up in all kinds of corners. May we all continue to read the word, write the word, and express ourselves with genuine words."